Four Steps to Peace

THE JOURNEY

By Carol Graves

Four Steps to Peace – The Journey
By Carol Graves
Design by Melody Warford
Cover Photograph by Laura Closner

Printed in the United States of America
Fully In Focus, San Antonio, Texas 78249

ISBN 13: 978-0-9830847-5-4
ISBN 10: 0983084750

Additional copies of this Bible Study can be ordered online at

www.fullyinfocus.com

e-mail fullyinfocus@yahoo.com

Contents *Introduction*

Prayer Journal

In the back pages of this book you will find a place to record your thoughts and prayers. In days and years to come, these journal entries will become "memorial stones" of a growing faith, showing the ways God has worked in response to prayer.

About the Author

Carol Graves is passionate in her desire to share how God has led her to a place of peace through focused prayer. As the leader of a prayer group for many years, she has experienced the life transforming power of focusing on the fullness of God.

In her desire to equip others to experience the peace and joy she has found through a knowledge of God's character, she has written two devotional books. Her first, *Fully In Focus – A Scriptural Collection Illustrating the Attributes of God* was recognized with a Christian Choice Book Award. Wanting to share even more of God's attributes, she wrote a second book, *Fully In Focus – Discovering the Fullness of God*. Each book features 52 attributes of God. The definitions, personal notes and Scripture references encourage a deeper knowledge of God's character.

Her passion for those of all ages to experience the fullness of God led her to write five children's books. Books for small children include *The Grumble Bug*, also recognized with a Christian Choice Book Award, *My First Glimpse of God - The Shining Star of Christmas*. These books, written in rhyme and illustrated with expressive stick figures, tell of God's character and goodness, encouraging a knowledge of God at an early age.

For young readers Carol has written two "chapter books." *The Girl Who Wanted a Friend* presents the message that Jesus invites us to be His friend, just the way we are. *The Boy Who Said "I Can't!"* teaches about courage, perseverance, and the wisdom of trusting God.

Carol is a retired school teacher with a wide variety of career experiences. Now she enjoys sharing her passion, speaking at retreats and sharing with various groups.

Carol is the mother of three children and grandmother of three. She lives with her husband, Dave, in San Antonio, Texas.

Introduction

Four Steps to Peace

The Journey

It was a very dark place with uncertainty surrounding me. It seemed that I was paralyzed with fear and doubt. Unable to take even one step forward, I stood there not knowing what to do. As my mind swirled with frightening thoughts, suddenly it landed on one that brought a glimpse of light and I spoke the word. "God." I had always known that God is near, but now He seemed far away. "God," I cried. "I need you!" Now my mind was flooded with new, more peaceful thoughts. God is here. God cares. God helps. God guides. God protects. God quiets. I felt calmed as I focused on God and my heart was filled with praise. I took one step toward peace.

Suddenly, thoughts of past mistakes pounded through my head. Guilt. Shame. Darkness dimmed the light that I had seen. I cried out once again, "God, I am sorry! Forgive me." As I spoke those words, the light became bright once again. Repentance brought a sense of relief and I was able to take a second step. Once again peace appeared and it was closer than it had been before.

Hope slipped gently into my mind and as it did I remembered things from the past that had given me encouragement. Healing. Provision. Safety. Forgiveness. Blessings. When I had spoken to God in prayer in the past, His answers were miraculous and always on time. It was as though I wanted to write a thank-you note to God, acknowledging all the ways He had worked in my life and in the lives of those I love. I spoke aloud saying, "Thank you, thank you, thank you!" As I did, I felt the sweet peace I sought once again filling my heart and illuminating my path.

As I took another step, suddenly my heart was filled with anxious thoughts. Needs. Fears. Relationships. Finances. Health. I struggled, trying to take another step, but once again I could not move. It was as though I had come to a giant wall that kept me from moving forward. The wall blocked the light that had kept me moving forward and I did not know what to do. I closed my eyes and breathed a simple prayer, "God, I know you are near. I know you are able to remove the wall that keeps me from your peace. I trust in You. I yield my fears and concerns to Your power and strength. Help me." I opened my eyes and the wall was gone. The room was full of light and I could see that there was nothing to fear. What had once been a dark and fearful place, now was a place of peace.

These four steps had taken me from darkness to peace.

Praise

With all my heart I will praise you, O LORD my God. I will give glory to your name forever. Psalm 86:12 (NLT)

Repent

Day and night your hand of discipline was heavy on me. My strength evaporated like water in the summer heat. Finally, I confessed all my sins to you and stopped trying to hide my guilt. I said to myself, "I will confess my rebellion to the LORD." And you forgave me! All my guilt is gone. Psalm 32:4-5 (NLT)

Acknowledge

Acknowledge that the LORD is God! He made us, and we are his. We are his people, the sheep of his pasture. Enter his gates with thanksgiving; go into his courts with praise. Give thanks to him and praise his name. For the LORD is good. His unfailing love continues forever, and his faithfulness continues to each generation. Psalm 100:3-5 (NLT)

Yield

Give all your worries and cares to God, for he cares about you. 1 Peter 5:7 (NLT)

Pray

Always be joyful. Never stop praying. Be thankful in all circumstances, for this is God's will for you who belong to Christ Jesus. 1 Thessalonians 5:16-18 (NLT)

Peace is that state of calm, freedom from strife or discord, rest of heart and mind that we all seek. In the next few weeks we will be taking a journey that leads to peace. The vehicle for this journey is prayer. The journey we will take together includes four simple steps, and the destination is sure. Let's start by focusing on the vehicle that will take us there – prayer.

What is Prayer?

In the dictionary "prayer" is defined as "a humble and sincere request to God; an utterance to God in praise, thanksgiving, confession; any spiritual communion with God." This definition comes surprisingly close to what we will study together in the next few weeks. We will examine four steps of prayer. Praise. Repent. Acknowledge. Yield. PRAY. Together we will experience how these steps take us on a journey that leads to peace. Let's get started!

Week One

Preparing for the Journey

As we start our journey to peace, just as with any journey, we must make sure that we are ready and headed in the right direction. This first week we will make sure that we are properly prepared.

Day One — *First Things First*

How can I know God hears my prayer?

This common question has a clear answer. It starts with a relationship. Think about the conversations you have every day. Perhaps you have a short conversation with someone at the grocery store or at work. You may talk with a neighbor or with someone on the phone. But usually these conversations are somewhat superficial. "How are you?" "Isn't this nice weather?" "We went to a great restaurant this weekend." Simple conversations like these are quickly forgotten. "In one ear and out the other," is an old saying that might describe these conversations.

The serious, important matters are usually discussed with those you trust. This might be family or close friends. You find these people trustworthy because you have developed a relationship with them. You know that they are willing to listen when you need to talk about your fears or failures. You seek their counsel and depend on their support and encouragement. Your relationship is not threatened by anything you might say.

In answer to the question, we can know that God hears our prayer if we have a relationship with Him. This leads to the most important question: "How do I know that I have a relationship with God?"

Hebrews 11:6 (The Message) states: *"It's impossible to please God apart from faith. And why? Because anyone who wants to approach God must believe both that he exists and that he cares enough to respond to those who seek him."*

According to this scripture, what is the first step in establishing a relationship with God?

_____

Several years ago I was telling a friend about my relationship with God. When I asked if she would like to invite God into her life she replied, "I just don't have the faith." According to the following scripture where does that faith come from?

_____

Ephesians 2:8-9 (NIV) *For it is by grace you have been saved, through faith—and this is not from yourselves, it is the gift of God— not by works, so that no one can boast.*

God used this verse to clearly show me how to establish a relationship with Him.

My Journey of Faith

The journey leading to my relationship with God began as a child. I knew about God and I knew that Jesus was the Son of God. I knew that there was a heaven and a hell. I knew that I wanted to go to heaven and I thought that I had to be "good enough" to get there. In my mind, there was a giant scale that weighed my good deeds and my bad deeds and only if the scale tipped to the good side would I make it to heaven. Although I tried hard to "work my way to heaven" I was fearful that I would not make it because I knew that I was not always good. The older I grew, the more fearful I became and the less sure I was of my final destination.

Then, about a year after I was married, a friend that I worked with invited me and my husband to a retreat. I remember that it was June, 1969. As we visited, she showed me the verse in the Bible, Ephesians 2:8-9, that said salvation is a free gift. That verse amazed me, because it clearly stated that I could not "work my way" to heaven. Somehow that seemed too easy and almost too good to be true. To consider that the grace of God freely given to me depended only on faith, not works, was different than I had ever known. What if it was true?

The next day at lunch a group of us sat together and one fellow asked, "Carol, how long have you been a Christian?"

I wasn't sure how to answer that question. I always thought that I could not call myself a Christian, for I was not sure that I was "good enough." I gave the best answer I could and told him that I had joined the church at age 12. He smiled, then said, "But that is not what I asked." Then he started drawing an illustration on a napkin. There were two cliffs separated by a large expanse. On one side he labeled "perfect/God" and the other side "sinful/man." He asked me, "Carol, which side are you on?"

I knew for sure that I was not perfect, but I had been "striving" trying to live a good life, so I answered, "I think I am somewhere in the middle."

He smiled and said, "I am sorry, but it is impossible to be in the middle. You are either on one side or the other."

Obviously he was right. I knew, however, that if I had to place myself on one side, it would have to be on the side of sinful man. It was then that he drew the "bridge" that closed the gap between God and man. It was in the shape of a cross and he wrote the word, "Jesus" on it. He explained that Jesus paid the price for my sin by his death on the cross, that he overcame death and rose again. By confessing my sin and believing in Him, he explained that I could freely cross over, enjoy a relationship with God and receive the promise of Heaven. The scriptures and that little illustration helped me see that, just as it was impossible to be suspended in mid-air between two cliffs, it was impossible to "work my way" to a relationship with God. The expanse between my sin and God's perfection was too great.

When he asked if I would like to pray to receive the gift of salvation, I was overjoyed. Without hesitation I responded, "Yes!" I prayed, I confessed that I am a sinner and asked God to forgive me. I invited Jesus Christ into my heart as my Savior. I received the gift of salvation and eternal life through faith in Jesus Christ. That day was the beginning of a growing relationship with God.

You know my story, now write your story. When did you receive the gift of salvation and become a friend of God? Write your story and share it with your group. If you are unsure of your story, continue reading and learn how you can receive the life-changing gift of salvation.

My Salvation Story

_____

_____

_____

_____

_____

_____

_____

If you have not received the free gift of salvation, your story can begin today. Romans 10:17 (NIV) says: _Consequently, faith comes from hearing the message, and the message is heard through the word about Christ._ The following scriptures from the New Living Translation of God's Word, the Bible, show us God's plan of salvation.

Romans 3:23 For everyone has sinned; we all fall short of God's glorious standard.

Romans 6:23 For the wages of sin is death, but the _free gift_ of God is eternal life through Christ Jesus our Lord.

Romans 5:8 But God showed his great love for us by sending Christ to die for us while we were still sinners.

Romans 10:9-10 If you confess with your mouth that Jesus is Lord and believe in your heart that God raised him from the dead, you will be saved. For it is by believing in your heart that you are made right with God, and it is by confessing with your mouth that you are saved.

Romans 10:13 For "Everyone who calls on the name of the LORD will be saved."

John 3:16 For God loved the world so much that he gave his one and only Son, so that everyone who believes in him will not perish but have eternal life.

God's Word explains that God loves you and wants to have a relationship with you. He loves you so much that He provides everything you need to establish that relationship. He provided His Son to pay the penalty for your sin. He has given you His Word to show the way of salvation. He gives the gift of faith that you might receive Jesus Christ as your Savior.

If you believe God's word and would like to invite Jesus Christ into your life as your Savior, pray a simple prayer similar to this:

God, I confess that I am a sinner. I believe that Jesus Christ died to pay the penalty for my sin. I want to know You and have a relationship with you. I ask you to come into my life. Teach me how to live my life for you. Thank you for my salvation. Amen.

Before I received Jesus Christ as my Savior, I was unsure of eternal life with God in heaven. If you have believed, prayed and received God's gift of salvation, His Word gives us this assurance:

1 John 5:13 (NLT) I have written this to you who believe in the name of the Son of God, so that you may know you have eternal life.

John 1:12 (NIV) Yet to all who did receive him, to those who believed in his name, he gave the right to become children of God.

Now you are a part of God's family. You can enjoy a relationship with God as His child. If you have received the gift of salvation, record the today's date and write your story, then share it with someone.

My Story of Salvation

On _____ I received Jesus Christ as my Savior.

_____

_____

_____

_____

_____

_____

_____

_____

Now with certainty we can answer the question, "How do we know that God hears our prayer?" Because we enjoy a relationship with Him, He listens to our cries and hears our prayer. Read from God's Word the assurance that God hears.

God Hears

Hear: to listen to and consider; to take notice of and pay attention to

According to the scripture, there is one thing that causes God to turn a deaf ear to our prayers - sin. Isaiah 59:2 says, *"But your iniquities have separated you from your God; your sins have hidden his face from you, so that he will not hear."* Yet in 1 John 1:9 we are encouraged: *"If we confess our sins, he is faithful and just and will forgive us our sins and purify us from all unrighteousness."* That confession of sin opens the heart of God to once again hear our prayers. The power of prayer is amazing as God listens and considers our petitions. God desires to release his blessings and guide our path as we seek him and voice our requests. God's word confirms that when we pray with a clean heart, God hears.

Psalm 4:3 Know that the LORD has set apart the godly for himself; the LORD will hear when I call to him.

Psalm 5:3 In the morning, O LORD, you hear my voice; in the morning I lay my requests before you and wait in expectation.

Psalm 6:9 The LORD has heard my cry for mercy; the LORD accepts my prayer.

Psalm 10:17 You hear, O LORD, the desire of the afflicted; you encourage them, and you listen to their cry.

Psalm 65:1-3 Praise awaits you, O God, in Zion; to you our vows will be fulfilled. O you who hear prayer, to you all men will come. When we were overwhelmed by sins, you forgave our transgressions.

Psalm 145:18-19 The LORD is near to all who call on him, to all who call on him in truth. He fulfills the desires of those who fear him; he hears their cry and saves them.

2 Chronicles 7:14 ...if my people, who are called by my name, will humble themselves and pray and seek my face and turn from their wicked ways, then will I hear from heaven and will forgive their sin and will heal their land.

1 John 5:14 This is the confidence we have in approaching God: that if we ask anything according to his will, he hears us.

Day Two — *Why Pray?*

Have you ever had a friend who, for some unknown reason, stopped speaking to you? How did that make you feel? When I was a young mother, busy taking care of two little ones, I had an experience that I still remember. We lived in a neighborhood between the homes of families who had lived there long before we arrived. These neighbors had long established friendships with each other. Although they were friendly and talked to me occasionally, I found it difficult to establish a relationship with them. Because we had only one car, I had little opportunity to go anywhere while my husband was at work and I became lonely. I longed to visit with my neighbors, but they did not seem interested in calling or visiting. I couldn't understand why they wouldn't take the time to call or visit with me. I remember standing at my sink in the kitchen as God spoke to my heart, "Now you know how I feel when you do not speak to me."

That thought broke my heart. It was true. I was so busy taking care of the children, keeping the house clean, doing laundry, cooking meals, and all of those other things that keep a young mother so busy, that I had not taken time to grow my relationship with God. He wanted to hear from me. He wanted to fellowship with me. He wanted to talk with me. He wanted me to pray.

Some ask the question, "Why pray?" Let's explore God's Word and find some answers.

God's Word

God's Word teaches us about prayer and instructs us to pray. Read each of the following scriptures and describe what each verse teaches about prayer.

Colossians 4:2 _____

Luke 18:1_____

1 Thessalonians 5:17_____

Philippians 4:6 _____

1 Samuel 12:23 How did the prophet Samuel consider the failure to pray?

_____

The Scriptures teach that we should pray, but what is prayer all about? Is it a religious ritual that we perform? Is it an exercise in thinking pleasant thoughts? Is it a way to get things we want or a way to impress others? The Scriptures teach us that prayer is the door we use to communicate with God and develop an intimate relationship with Him.

Prayer Connects God and Man

As we draw near to God in prayer, our relationship with Him grows closer.

Romans 5:11 (NLT) *So now we can rejoice in our wonderful new relationship with God because our Lord Jesus Christ has made us friends of God.*

According to this scripture, what is our relationship with God?

_____

Psalm 17:6 (NIV) *I call on you, O God, for you will answer me; give ear to me and hear my prayer.*

With the technology that is available today, we have the ability to communicate as never before. Yet, how often does your phone ring and you look to see who is calling and turn off the phone. Often we answer our calls only when it is convenient – even if it is our friend who calls. According to this scripture, when we call, God

_____.

Psalm 10:17 (NIV) *You, LORD, hear the desire of the afflicted; you encourage them, and you listen to their cry.* Our relationship with God grows as we cry out to Him for help. This scripture shows that God listens and _____.

Psalm 54:4 (NIV) *Surely God is my help; the Lord is the one who sustains me.*

As our relationship grows through prayer, we realize that He is the One who will always

_____ and_____.

In week two we will focus on many of the attributes of God's character. Knowing who He is transforms our relationship with God dramatically. The more you know Him, the more you want to make Him known.

God Responds

Read **Matthew 7:7-11**

What action does this passage emphasizes about prayer?

_____

Read the following scriptures and fill in the blanks.

According to **Matthew 6:8b** (NLT) …your Father knows exactly what you need _____

_____.

Jeremiah 33:3 (NLT) Ask me and I will tell you _____ about

things to come.

Ephesians 3:20 (NLT) Now all glory to God, who is able, through his mighty power at

work within us, to accomplish infinitely more _____

_____.

James 1:5-7 (NLT) If you need wisdom, ask our generous God, and he will give it to

you. He will not rebuke you for asking. But when you ask him,_____

_____. Do not waver, for a person with divided loyalty

is as unsettled as a wave of the sea that is blown and tossed by the wind. Such people

should not expect to receive anything from the Lord.

Isaiah 65:1 (NLT) The LORD says, "I was ready to respond, but no one asked for help.

I was ready to be found, but no one was looking for me. I said, '_____

_____' to a nation that did not call on my name."

God wants to respond to our prayers, but first we must ask. What reason(s) would

cause you to hesitate to ask?_____

_____

_____

Jesus' Example

There are many accounts in the Scriptures of those who prayed to God including Moses, Sampson, Hannah, Samuel, David, Elijah, Solomon, and the list could go on and on. Perhaps the best example of one who prayed is Jesus Christ, himself.

When the disciples asked him how to pray, Jesus gave them instructions concerning prayer. Read **Matthew 6:5-15**. Here he teaches them how to pray. Commonly known as the Lord's Prayer, this sample prayer includes the elements of prayer that we will explore in this study. In the blanks that follow, write the phrase that suggests these elements of prayer:

Praise _____

Repentance _____

Acknowledgement _____

Yield _____

In verses 14-15, what condition does Jesus require when we ask God to forgive our sin?

_____

_____

The ministry of Jesus was extensive and demanding. In the New Testament we read many accounts of His teaching, ministering, healing and reaching out to those who needed His touch. In one account, Jesus had just preached to masses of people and miraculously fed the 5.000. Surely He must have been exhausted. Read **Mark 6:45-46**.

What did Jesus do at the close of the day?_____

Jesus Prays

The following Scriptural accounts describe some of the final prayers Jesus prayed before His death and resurrection.

Read **John 17:1-26** This is referred to as The Prayer of Jesus.

Jesus prayed this prayer after teaching His disciples privately just before His arrest and death. In it we see that Jesus and God are One. Jesus expresses His desire to bring glory to God and his deep love for the disciples and for all future believers. He prays for our protection, that we may have a full measure of His joy, that we will experience unity as believers and that we will be set apart by His truth. This prayer was prayed for you.

Read **Matthew 26:36-42**

After teaching the disciples and sharing The Last Supper Jesus went with His disciples to the pray in the Garden of Gethsemane. Here we see the beginning of the anguish Jesus suffered as He faced the cross alone.

What did Jesus pray in both verse 39 and verse 42?_____

_____

_____

In Luke 23:34a (NLT) Jesus prays a short prayer while dying on the cross: Jesus said, "*Father, forgive them, for they don't know what they are doing.*"

Through His death on the cross, Jesus paid the penalty for sin once and for all. He claimed victory over sin and by His resurrection He claimed victory over death. Even as He died, He prayed for you and me.

Prayer Brings Joy

Some may ask why we often close prayer with the phrase "in Jesus name we pray." In John 16:22-24 (NLT) Jesus tells us the answer. *"So you have sorrow now, but I will see you again; then you will rejoice, and no one can rob you of that joy. At that time you won't need to ask me for anything. I tell you the truth, you will ask the Father directly, and he will grant your request because you use my name. You haven't done this before. Ask, using my name, and you will receive, and you will have abundant joy."*

We pray in Jesus' name for He is The Way that we come into a relationship with God. It is because of Him that we can freely come before the presence of God in prayer. It is in the presence of God that we find true joy. God's Word says it best:

Psalm 16:11 (NIV) *You make known to me the path of life; you will fill me with joy in your presence, with eternal pleasures at your right hand.*

Why Pray?

List some reasons from this study that answer the question, "Why pray?" _____

_____

_____

_____

_____

_____

_____

_____

Day Three   How do I pray?

What is prayer? Prayer is a conversation with God. When we pray it is more than talking to God, it is talking with God. Through the privilege of prayer we can interact with the Creator of the Universe – think of it! As shown throughout the Scriptures, these conversations with God are powerful. We are just ordinary people praying extraordinary prayers that can impact the lives of many – for generations to come.

A prayer can be a long conversation with God or as short as one word. It can be spoken out loud, whispered or communicated silently. It can be spoken privately, with a prayer partner or in a group setting.

Prayers can be spoken at specific times or the conversation with God can continue endlessly throughout the day or night. Read **1 Thessalonians 5:17**.

What simple instruction does this give us about how often we should pray? _____

_____

Although there are no "rules" that we must follow when we pray, there are certain aspects of prayer that enhance one's prayer life. Today we will explore conversational prayer. At first, this may seem uncomfortable to some because conversational prayer refers to prayer that is shared between two or more who are praying out loud.

How do you feel about praying out loud in the following situations: (willing or unwilling)

with a family member _____

with a friend _____

with a prayer partner _____

in a small group _____

leading pray in a large group setting _____

Some feel reluctant to pray out loud in any situation. What factors might contribute to this feeling? _____

_____

Many times we are reluctant to pray out loud because we feel that others might judge us either for the manner in which we pray or for the needs that we pray for. We fear that praying out loud might open up our lives to others in ways that might be embarrassing. That fear is a result of pride and pride is one of the tools the enemy uses to keep us from living a victorious life.

Parable of the Private Passengers

The couple stood together awaiting the call to board the huge yacht anchored at the dock. They were full of excitement as they walked onboard, ready to take a wonderful journey. Never having taken such a trip before, the first thing the couple did was to find their quarters. As they moved to the deck below, they were comforted by the sight of the Captain at the controls of their yacht and they felt confident and excited about their journey.

They entered their cabin, and were surprised to find that the space was somewhat confining and different than they had imagined it would be. But making the necessary adjustments, they decided to take a nap and closed the door to their cabin. Their dream had come true and they were ready to enjoy a very pleasant journey.

As the yacht went out to sea, a sudden storm awakened them with a jolt. The passengers found themselves thrown to the floor of their cabin and their yacht seemed to be swaying to and fro with the sound of splashing and strong winds outside. The yacht seemed out of control. This was not what they had hoped for - this was not a part of their plan. They feared that their journey would be ruined and that all their dreams and expectations would not be fulfilled.

Just as the yacht rolled far on its side, there came a soft knock on the door of the cabin. "This is the Captain," spoke a calm gentle voice. "Are you all right?" Not wanting to appear frightened, they confidently said, "Oh, everything is just fine in here." The voice of the Captain continued, "We have run into quite a storm, but don't worry, I have everything under control. We will come through the storm safely. If there is anything you need, just call me and I will be right here to help you."

Rather than calming down, the storm became even stronger. Having never experienced such rough seas, the passengers began to feel very sick. They remembered how they had dreamed of a wonderful journey and this was certainly not what they had hoped. Afraid, alone and confined, they decided the best thing to do was just to stay in their cabin with their door shut tight. Although they were extremely uncomfortable, they did not want to call on their Captain, fearing that he was too busy trying to keep the yacht on course.

The hours turned to days and the storm continued to rage. The passengers were afraid to open the door of their cabin. They were very apprehensive about what they would find outside their door, so it seemed much safer just to keep the door shut and stay inside. It was a sudden shriek that pierced through the storm that caused the sick and desperate passengers to bolt to their door. "Man overboard!" came the urgent cry. The couple flung open the door of their cabin and as they looked out they gazed into the frightened faces of multitudes of others just like them. Almost in unison the passengers exclaimed, "We're all in the same boat!" Because each of the couples had immediately gone to their cabin and closed the door when they boarded for the journey no one knew that there were many others experiencing the same storm. Now they discovered that they were not alone.

"If only we had opened our doors sooner we could have comforted each other and faced the storm together," they thought. Their desperate needs erased all embarrassment of having been so afraid. The passengers immediately began to help each other. Some took care of the sick, some prepared food, some spoke encouraging words to those who were especially frightened, some bailed water from the deck and some tried to rescue the one who had fallen overboard.

The storm raged on but it seemed to be less frightening because they were all riding it out together. Yet time was running out and it appeared that the trip would end in tragedy unless they were saved from the storm. One of the passengers remembered the words of the Captain and asked if any of the others had heard his message. One by one the passengers remembered the Captain's words. He had knocked on each of their doors. Joining their voices they called to him, "Captain! Captain! We need you! Save us from the storm! Please, save us!"

The Captain was immediately by their side, guiding them to safe areas of the yacht and calming their fears. The Captain assured them that there was no storm too strong for him to handle and that they could rest knowing that even though the storm seemed severe, the ship was still under his control. He promised that they would be safe.

After a time, the rain and the winds stopped, the sun came out from behind the clouds, and the passengers were amazed at how the Captain had brought them safely through the terrible storm. They thanked him again and again for saving them. They even spoke to each other about how they felt when they were alone, shut in their cabin and how much better they felt when they knew that they were not alone. Amazingly, they agreed that the journey had turned out even better than they had ever dreamed and as they departed the yacht they went straight to the booking office to sign up for another journey. This time, however, they all asked for cabins which had no doors and would accept no other Captain than the one who had delivered them from the storm.

It seemed that the passengers no longer wanted to be private. They wanted to share their journey with all the others. They had discovered that the best part of the journey was the relationship and support they had shared as they went through the storm. They all agreed that getting to know their very capable Captain was the highlight of the journey. Oh, and one more thing. They realized that had it not been for the storm, they might still be just a bunch of private passengers.

This parable illustrates the journey of life when often our experiences do not match our expectations. The storm represents difficulties we commonly face.

When their expectations of the journey were not met, what was the emotional response of the passengers? _____

_____

What was their physical response? _____

Have you faced difficulties that you were unwilling or embarrassed to share with others?

_____

_____

At this point the situation worsened. What change did the severity of the storm bring about among the passengers? _____

_____

All too often we feel that we are alone – that we are the only one facing difficulties. This feeling of loneliness is enhanced when we shut ourselves in and face our fears alone. In reality, we all face similar problems. In the parable, what did the passengers say when they opened their doors and discovered that they were not alone on the yacht?

_____

Yes, we are all in the same boat. We have similar problems, similar challenges and similar fears. How did the passengers respond to each other as they faced the storm?

_____

When the Captain first came to check on the passengers, what was their response?

_____

How did the attitude of the passengers change toward the Captain and why?

_____

_____

_____

Who was in control during the storm? _____

Who do you think the Captain represents in the parable?

_____

_____

During the journey the passengers opened up to each other and came to know and trust the Captain. All of this came about because of the _____.

Does the message of this parable apply to your life? _____

In what way? _____

_____

_____

_____

_____

Beware

The Scriptures warn us that we have an enemy. This enemy tries to use the storms in our life to isolate us and draw us away from God. 1 Peter 5:8 (NLT) *Stay alert! Watch out for your great enemy, the devil. He prowls around like a roaring lion, looking for someone to devour.* This enemy knows the power of prayer and will use any deception to keep us from effectively praying together.

When storms come in your life, God wants you to call out to Him. We find hope in Jesus' words from Matthew 11:28 (NLT) *Come to me all of you who are weary and carry heavy burdens, and I will give you rest.*

God calls us to pray for one another, yet how can that happen if we are unwilling to share our needs? The truth is found in God's Word. 1 Corinthians 12:26 (NLT) *If one part suffers, all the parts suffer with it, and if one part is honored, all the parts are glad.*

Conversational Prayer

Conversational prayer is exactly that – a conversation with God. When you are praying out loud with a prayer partner, you converse with God just as you do with each other. In a conversation, usually a simple question or statement strikes up a dialogue that goes back and forth with questions and responses. When two or more are praying in a conversational manner, it is the same. One may pray a phrase and the other may pray a simple statement of agreement or pray another request. Conversational prayer is a back and forth conversation with God and your prayer partner.

Gathering to pray out loud might be scary at first but remember, you are having a conversation with God, not performing for man. God is anxious to hear your prayers and He does not give you a score on your wording or presentation.

As we unite in prayer, faith is multiplied. When you hear your prayer partner praying the words that you could not voice yourself, you begin to see the power of the Holy Spirit. Not only is faith increased, but those who are praying are surrounded by a loving spirit of unity, all believing in the faithfulness of God.

There are times when your heart is so heavy you simply don't know what to pray. Even then we find help in Romans 8: 26-27 (NLT) *And the Holy Spirit helps us in our weakness. For example, we don't know what God wants us to pray for. But the Holy Spirit prays for us with groanings that cannot be expressed in words. And the Father who knows all hearts knows what the Spirit is saying, for the Spirit pleads for us believers in harmony with God's own will.*

When words cannot be spoken, God knows our heart and the Holy Spirit intercedes for us.

Confidentiality

One last consideration about conversational prayer is the importance of confidentiality. Conversational prayer is not a source of information to discuss with others. A true prayer partner is one who can be trusted to keep prayer requests confidential unless given permission to share with others. The only reason they should be shared with permission is to ask others to join in prayer.

> Nothing tends more to cement the hearts of Christians than praying together. Never do they love one another so well as when they witness the outpouring of each other's hearts in prayer.
>
> *- Charles Finney*

One Accord Prayer   Day Four

What is One Accord Prayer?

One accord prayer is Holy Spirit directed prayer where two or more agree. Jesus speaks of this in Matthew 18:19-20 (NLT) *I also tell you this: If two of you agree here on earth concerning anything you ask, my Father in heaven will do it for you. For where two or three gather together as my followers, I am there among them.*

The power of one accord prayer is demonstrated in that two or more are praying in agreement in the presence of God. One accord prayer is exponential in nature. In math, an exponent placed after a number indicates its "power." The number 10 can be raised in power by adding an exponent. The number 10^2 is 10x10=100, but the number 10^3 is 10x10x10=1000. In this illustration, each increase of the exponent by just one number multiplies the amount of the number times itself. Imagine how the power of prayer is multiplied when many pray in agreement! Never underestimate the power of one accord prayer.

Why Pray Together?

What do the following Scriptures say about praying together in one accord?

Matthew 18:20 _____

_____

_____

Galatians 6:2 _____

_____

_____

Matthew 18:19 _____

_____

_____

1 Thessalonians 5:11 _____

_____

_____

The power of prayer is multiplied when people unite in prayer. Hearing another praying in faith for your need causes hope to spring forth. God's power is experienced in a new way. A strong cord of faith consisting of three strands - you, your prayer partner and God becomes a powerful weapon against the enemy.

Ecclesiastes 4:12 (NIV) *Though one may be overpowered, two can defend themselves. A cord of three strands is not quickly broken.*

The Power of One Accord Prayer Demonstrated

In Acts 1:13-14 (NKJ) we read about those who gathered together to pray after Jesus ascended to the Father. *And when they had entered, they went up into the upper room where they were staying: Peter, James, John, and Andrew; Philip and Thomas; Bartholomew and Matthew; James the son of Alphaeus and Simon the Zealot; and Judas the son of James. These all continued with one accord in prayer and supplication, with the women and Mary the mother of Jesus, and with His brothers.*

The power of one accord prayer is demonstrated in Acts 2. Peter and the eleven apostles preached with the power of the Holy Spirit.

Read **Acts 2:41**. What happened when they finished preaching?

_____

_____

Read **Acts 2:42** What did the new believers devote themselves to? _____

_____

_____

_____

Examples of One Accord Prayer

Summarize the requests made in the following "one accord" prayers and the results of those prayers:

Acts 4:23-31 _____

_____

_____

Acts 12:5-12 _____

_____

Acts 16:25-34 _____

_____

_____

These accounts demonstrate why we pray together in one accord. We also find encouragement in Hebrews 4:16 (NLT) _So let us come boldly to the throne of our gracious God. There we will receive his mercy, and we will find grace to help us when we need it most._

Modern technology allows our prayer requests to be made known quickly and globally. It allows us to communicate the prayer requests to prayer warriors and their prayers to those for whom we pray. The following account illustrates how one accord prayer gave me the opportunity to become a part of something much bigger.

Blake's Story

Friday, August 6, 2010 - I received a tearful, desperate call from my sister-in-law. She told me that their grandson, Blake, was near death and asked us to pray. A 15 year old boy with special needs, Blake was being discharged from the hospital after corrective foot surgery. His release was delayed and as they waited for the final word to go home, Blake went to sleep. Without warning, he stopped breathing and immediately his body systems started shutting down. He was admitted to ICU and placed on life support. The doctors advised that his condition was critical and he might not survive. To allow his body to rest, the doctors induced a coma. The family was devastated.

After this call, I immediately sent e-mails to family and several moms I pray with regularly. I explained the situation and asked them to join me in prayer. Having prayed with these women for many years, I knew that in one accord they would join in the battle for Blake's life. The prayer responses to my e-mails started pouring in. I immediately forwarded each e-mail to Blake's father and to my brother.

Sunday, August 8 – This message was forwarded to those who were praying: "*I received a message from the family. The doctor said Blake has come light years from where he was. He is still sedated and in critical condition, but his systems have started functioning. He will be sedated for another 48 hours at least to give his body rest allowing time for the systems to recover.*"

August 10 - In response to this news I received the following e-mail from one of the prayer warriors: "*I celebrate the goodness of the LORD with you in the change in Blake's status. What a ray of hope for the family. What an answer to prayer. God is able! I am so thankful. Thank you for telling me and encouraging my heart. We will press on in Jesus' name!*" Not only was God demonstrating His healing power in Blake's body, He was encouraging those who joined in the battle.

That same day I received an update and e-mailed it to the many who were praying: "*Thank you for your continued prayers for Blake. He continues to improve and at 8:00 am Wednesday morning the doctor will attempt to remove the respirator. This is a critical procedure due to the fact that Blake, due to his special needs condition, does not understand all the tubes and IV's and wants to pull them out. He has been sedated throughout his stay in ICU but the sedation must be decreased in order for him to breathe on his own. The doctor will be administering another drug to try to keep him calm as he removes the respirator.*

Please pray that Blake's body will respond favorably to the drugs administered and that he will remain calm. Please pray that Blake will be able to breathe without the respirator. Please pray for the doctor as he does this procedure that he will draw on God's wisdom and direction.

His grandmother tearfully asked me to thank you for your prayers for Blake. She said there is no way they could ever thank the many who have prayed for Blake and the family and they are filled with praise to God for hearing the prayers of so many and sustaining Blake's life."

August 11 - The morning of the procedure I prayed this scripture and sent it to the family: "*Do not withhold your mercy from Blake, O Lord; may your love and your truth always protect Blake.*" Psalm 40:11

August 12 - I received this message from Blake's father: "*The plan to take him off the ventilator / life support didn't go well yesterday. The doctor has taken him off all the sedatives and all paralyzing drugs hoping he will respond and wake up. This hasn't happened yet. Blake has to be somewhat conscious to be taken off the ventilator. The doctor has said all his organs are in good shape. The only concern is his brain activity. It is unknown why he isn't regaining consciousness. Please, Please continue to pray that Blake will awaken and that his brain activity will be normal. I can not express how much we appreciate your prayers!!*"

The communication between the parents, myself, and the prayer warriors continued as I relayed the messages by e-mail. Each and every message about Blake's condition was forwarded to the prayer warriors and their prayers and responses were forwarded to the family. The knowledge that people were praying was vital to the family during the time of crisis. Blake remained in a coma, then once again I received an update.

August 16 – "*Last time I posted, Blake's doctor felt he was progressing well enough to wean Blake off of sedation so that they could take out his breathing tube. Last Wednesday, they started this process, and as of Wednesday night, Blake was not showing any signs of waking up. Going into Thursday, the medical staff was telling us to stay patient because he had been so sedated. By Thursday evening, Blake's doctor seemed worried and ordered neurological testing. After this, the neurologist confirmed* that Blake was in a coma and had suffered some brain damage. At this time, our world came crashing down once again. They said at that time, there was nothing more they could do but wait and hope for his brain to improve versus the alternative. They also advised that if he did come out of the coma, they could not yet say what his brain function would be. Once again, by the miraculous Grace of God, by late Friday night, Blake was starting to show signs of movement. By Saturday, Blake was starting to move his eyes. Although extremely weak, early Sunday morning, Blake's doctor felt that his improvement was so great that he was ready to take him off the ventilator. By Sunday night, Blake was showing signs of his own personality. He was motioning for me to put my hair down and take my glasses off! When I did, he got so excited and, although not making any sound yet, smiled and laughed really big. I thought I would faint! I was witnessing a miracle. They are going to try to allow him to sit up in a wheel chair today, which will make him happy, and also because he has some "junk" in his lungs that they are trying to diminish, in order to prevent pneumonia. Thank you all, once again, for your support, your phone calls, your visits, and especially your prayers."

This good news brought a sweet response from one of the prayer warriors. "Shaking my tambourine over the huge miracle of life God has given to Blake and the hope and joy that knows no bounds for you and your family. Oh, how He loves us!" I forwarded it to the family. What an example of joy for those who are prayed for as well as those who pray!

August 20 – I sent this e-mail to the prayer warriors, "Blake is on his way home from the hospital! His grandmother just called and I could hear the huge smile as she spoke. Blake is still weak and will need to take breathing treatments until his lungs clear up, but he continues to improve each day. What an incredible, awesome miracle God has shown us. What a testimony to the power of God and the power of prayer! Thank you again for being a part of this miracle!"

September 16 – After continued prayer, I received another message from Blake's family. "I just wanted to share this picture with all of you that Blake's teacher posted on facebook, today. Looking at this picture of Blake with his friends, back at school, just took my breath and made me cry. (Happy cry, of course!) It is just such a wonderful reminder of God's miracles. Just one month ago, we thought we would have to say good-bye to Blake, and there he is back at school, learning and growing. Thank you, God!"

Blake's story is a vivid example of the power of one accord prayer. God heard our prayers and healed Blake completely. He shows no adverse effects of the ordeal. I praise God for the way he worked a miracle in our family as he brought Blake back to us.

Some might say that individuals with severe special needs have no purpose in life. One of the first messages I received from my brother at the very beginning of this crisis suggests otherwise. This was his prayer: "We are praying that God will reveal Himself in a mighty way as he brings Blake to full recovery. Even though Blake is limited as a person, he has affected so many lives and is known by more people than I could know. Dear friends, thank you for your prayers for our little man. We love him so very much."

When we have a relationship with God, when we share our concerns and needs, when we join in one accord prayer, miracles can happen. God not only works in the life of those we pray for, He works in our lives as well causing our faith to grow and our joy to increase as we see His response to our prayers. This experience is one that our family and those who prayed will never forget. It has become a marker in our lives of God's love and care for His children.

God's Word is Powerful

When we bring God's Word into our prayer,
we bring His power into our prayer.

- Joni Erickson Tada

In Genesis chapter 1, we read the first account of the power of God's spoken word. What words precede each act of creation?

_____

In the same way that God's spoken word is powerful, so is His written word. 2 Timothy 3:16a (NLT) states, *All Scripture is inspired by God. Just as God spoke all creation into being, he breathed His Word into the heart of man who recorded it so that we could know God.*

Power Over Sin

When we read Jesus' prayer in John 17:15-16 (NLT), He prays, "*I'm not asking you to take them out of the world, but to keep them safe from the evil one. They do not belong to this world any more than I do.*"

Here, Jesus refers to "the world" and indicates that this is where the evil one dwells.

In 1 John 2:16 (NLT) we read, *For the world offers only a craving for physical pleasure, a craving for everything we see, and pride in our achievements and possessions. These are not from the Father, but are from this world.*

In this passage, we see three points of sin that the world offers. Some would say that Jesus did not face the temptations that we face today. The Scripture states that Jesus was tempted in "every way - just as we are. According to the Scripture, what are three basic points of temptation that are the root of every sin.

1) _____

2) _____

3(_____

Jesus adds to His prayer in John 17:17 *Make them holy by your truth; teach them your word, which is truth.* Jesus knew the power of the Word of God. He knew that the truth of God's Word is the weapon that can defeat the enemy.

The Temptation of Jesus

The account found in Matthew 4 illustrates how Jesus used the power of God's Word when tempted by Satan.

Read **Matthew 4:1-3** What point of temptation was represented by Satan's challenge?

_____

With what did Jesus respond in verse 4? _____

Read **Deuteronomy 8:3**

Read **Matthew 4:5-6** What point of temptation did this challenge represent? _____

_____

What did Satan use to add to the temptation? _____

Read **Psalms 91:11-12**

This shows that even the enemy knows God's Word. With his cunning nature he tries every way possible to lead us into sin.

Read **Matthew 4:7** With what did Jesus respond? _____

Read **Deuteronomy 6:16** Why do you think Satan preceded the first two challenges

with the phrase, "If you are the Son of God?" _____

_____

What did Jesus establish in his response? _____

_____

Read **Matthew 4:8-9** What does Satan imply in verse 9? _____

_____

What point of temptation does this challenge represent? _____

_____

What did Jesus command in verse 10? _____

Once again Jesus responded to Satan with the Word of God. Read **Deuteronomy 6:13a** and write the scripture he quoted.

_____

_____

What happened in **Matthew 4:11**? _____

_____

In what way were the Scriptures fulfilled in this verse? _____

_____

The account in Matthew is the basis for God's Word found in Hebrews 4:15 *For we do not have a high priest who is unable to empathize with our weaknesses, but we have one who has been tempted in every way, just as we are —yet he did not sin.*

Jesus was ready to respond to the enemy with an effective weapon. This shows the value of memorizing scripture. When we know God's Word we can appropriate its power in our lives.
Psalm 119:11 *I have hidden your word in my heart that I might not sin against you.*

Power Over the Enemy

When we pray we are engaging in combat with the enemy. God's Word gives us instruction about how to use His armor.

Read **Ephesians 6:10-17**

This passage of Scripture teaches us how to stand against the enemy. Verse 12 identifies

the enemy. It states that the battles we face are not against _____,

but are _____ in nature. All too often we are not focused on the true enemy.

List what the parts of the armor of God represent as found in Verses 13-17.

Belt represents _____

Body armor (breastplate) represents _____

Shoes represent _____

Shield represents _____

Helmet represents _____

Sword represents _____

Notice that most of the armor is defensive in nature. Which part of the armor is the

only offensive weapon against the enemy? _____

_____

Jesus chose the most powerful weapon in His battle with the enemy. He used God's Word. We can use Scripture in this same way. Praying Scripture is powerful as well as comforting as we speak God's Word.

Pray with Confidence

When we pray Scripture, we can know that we are praying according to God's will because we are praying His Word. This should instill a confidence within us as we lift up our prayers.

Read **Hebrews 4:16** According to this verse, we can come before God in what manner?

_____

1 John 3:21-22 (NLT) *Dear friends, if we don't feel guilty, we can come to God with bold confidence. And we will receive from him whatever we ask because we obey him and do the things that please him.*

What two conditions are suggested in this verse that might cause us to lack the bold confidence when we come before God?

1) _____

2) _____

1 John 5:14-15 (NIV) *This is the confidence we have in approaching God: that if we ask anything according to his will, he hears us. And if we know that he hears us—whatever we ask—we know that we have what we asked of him.*

In this verse, what condition is required for God to hear our prayer?

_____

All too often we pray according to what we think is best. We do not recognize that our limited understanding of the purposes of God can cause our prayers to reflect selfish motives and desires. When we are praying according to scripture under the direction of the Holy Spirit, we will pray according to God's will, not our own, and our requests will be granted. The many examples of prayer in the Bible make it clear that God responds positively when we pray in accordance with His will. After all, God knows what is best for us and we can trust Him to act accordingly.

There are times when we simply do not know what to pray. When we pray Scripture, we are praying God's Word. When we pray His Word, we are praying according to His will and we can confidently know that He hears us.

Ready for the First Step

We have spent the past five days preparing to start the journey to peace. First we explored the importance of establishing a relationship with God. Next we studied what God's Word teaches about prayer and looked at examples of the prayers of Jesus. We also learned about ways to enhance our prayer life through one accord prayer and conversational prayer. Last, we discovered that we can pray with confidence when we use God's Word in prayer.

Now that we are prepared for the journey, let us take the first step to peace.

Week Two

Starting the Journey
Praise

In the first week of this study we established that prayer is the vehicle that will take us on the journey as we travel to peace. Now as we take the first step in our journey, we will consider the importance of being clearly focused on God. As His character is revealed in the Scriptures and we begin to understand His fullness, peace will begin to pour into our hearts.

Day One   Why Praise?

Although prayer has been a part of my life as long as I remember, it was not until much later in life that I experienced the power of focused prayer. All too often my prayers were more like a "laundry list" of random needs, expressions of concern, even demands that I poured out to God, expecting Him to "take care" of the things that bothered me.

I will always remember one prayer when I was angry with God. I had always dreamed of becoming a mother and the possibility of that dream coming to reality seemed to be fading away. As I stood in my back yard, I remember angrily calling out to God, "Why? Why have you given me this strong desire to become a mother and not given me a child? This isn't fair!" I remember the almost immediate answer to that prayer. As I visualized how God's Son, Jesus Christ, died on the cross to pay the penalty for *my* sin, God gently spoke to my heart, *"And this was not fair."*

What right did I have to make demands of God? The truth remained that whether I ever had a child or not, God loved me and wanted the very best for me. God had a plan and loved me enough to fulfill His plan designed perfectly for me. I was humbled. I was changed. That day a journey began that has taken years to bring me to this point. That moment of humility began to show me how great God is and planted a seed of praise that began to grow.

The Starting Point

This first step in our journey is the most important. Rather than coming before God only when we are fearful or seek forgiveness, the first step in our journey is praise.

Today we will take time to explore scriptures that illustrate how praising God brings joy, both to Him and to us. As you read each Scripture you will begin to catch a glimpse of God's character. You will begin to see the loving, compassionate nature of God. You will find that the scriptures will reveal many answers to the question, "Why praise?"

Read each verse and underline the phrases that illustrate why God deserves our praise.

Exodus 15:2 The LORD is my strength and my song; he has given me victory. This is my God, and I will praise him—my father's God, and I will exalt him!

Deuteronomy 10:21 He alone is your God, the only one who is worthy of your praise, the one who has done these mighty miracles that you have seen with your own eyes.

2 Samuel 22:47 The LORD lives! Praise to my Rock! May God, the Rock of my salvation, be exalted!

1 Chronicles 16:24-26 Publish his glorious deeds among the nations. Tell everyone about the amazing things he does. Great is the LORD! He is most worthy of praise! He is to be feared above all gods. The gods of other nations are mere idols, but the LORD made the heavens!

1 Chronicles 16:36 Praise the LORD, the God of Israel, who lives from everlasting to everlasting! And all the people shouted "Amen!" and praised the LORD.

1 Chronicles 29:12-14 Wealth and honor come from you alone, for you rule over everything. Power and might are in your hand, and at your discretion people are made great and given strength. "O our God, we thank you and praise your glorious name! But who am I, and who are my people, that we could give anything to you? Everything we have has come from you, and we give you only what you first gave us!

Psalm 42:11 Why am I discouraged? Why is my heart so sad? I will put my hope in God! I will praise him again—my Savior and my God!

Psalm 56:4 I praise God for what he has promised. I trust in God, so why should I be afraid? What can mere mortals do to me?

Psalm 66:20 Praise God, who did not ignore my prayer or withdraw his unfailing love from me.

Psalm 68:19 Praise the Lord; praise God our savior! For each day he carries us in his arms.

Isaiah 25:1 O LORD, I will honor and praise your name, for you are my God. You do such wonderful things! You planned them long ago, and now you have accomplished them.

2 Corinthians 1:3 All praise to God, the Father of our Lord Jesus Christ. God is our merciful Father and the source of all comfort.

Ephesians 1:3 All praise to God, the Father of our Lord Jesus Christ, who has blessed us with every spiritual blessing in the heavenly realms because we are united with Christ.

Ephesians 1:6 So we praise God for the glorious grace he has poured out on us who belong to his dear Son.

Ephesians 1:14 The Spirit is God's guarantee that he will give us the inheritance he promised and that he has purchased us to be his own people. He did this so we would praise and glorify him.

Through the Scriptures we see why God is worthy of our praise. Although praising God brings Him glory, it has a profound effect on us as we praise Him. We have seen glimpses of His character through these Scriptures, but now, to fully comprehend His greatness, we must study His attributes.

All glory to him who alone is God, our Savior through Jesus Christ our Lord. All glory, majesty, power, and authority are his before all time, and in the present, and beyond all time! Amen. Jude 1:25 (NLT)

Day Two — *Getting to Know Him*

Praise is not thanking God for what He has done. It springs from knowing who He is. True praise starts with knowing the character of God. When we praise God we acknowledge His greatness. We come before Him with humility accepting that God can do what we cannot. We acknowledge His infinite wisdom. We express in words the ways that God is superior to man. We reflect on who God is and how limitless His resources are to meet our needs. We give glory – worshipful adoration – to God. All of this is praise. A study of His attributes results in true praise.

Through the years as I have traveled this journey to peace, I have been blessed as I studied the scriptures that illustrate the attributes of God. There are so many it is hard to know where to start, but one way to focus on the attributes of God is simply to go through the alphabet listing some of His attributes. With each attribute listed you will find a definition to further enhance your understanding and appreciation of the character of God. As we do this together, clear your mind of distractions and focus on God. You will find that praise comes very easily as you catch a glimpse of the fullness of God.

The Attributes of God

Read the following Scriptures that illustrate some of God's attributes. Write your expressions of praise in the blanks or add other attributes that come to mind.

A *God is Able* - having sufficient power, intelligence, competence, skill to accomplish action

Ephesians 3:20-21 Now to him who is able to do immeasurably more than all we ask or imagine, according to his power that is at work within us, to him be glory in the church and in Christ Jesus throughout all generations, for ever and ever! Amen.

_____

_____

_____

B *God is Boundless* - having no bounds; unlimited

Romans 11:33-36 Oh, the depth of the riches of the wisdom and knowledge of God! How unsearchable his judgments, and his paths beyond tracing out! Who has known the mind of the Lord? Or who has been his counselor? Who has ever given to God, that God should repay him? For from him and through him and to him are all things. To him be the glory forever! Amen.

C *God is Compassionate* - showing loving sympathy; sorrow for the trouble of others accompanied by an urge to help

Psalm 103:1-5 Praise the LORD, O my soul; all my inmost being, praise his holy name. Praise the LORD, O my soul, and forget not all his benefits -- who forgives all your sins and heals all your diseases, who redeems your life from the pit and crowns you with love and compassion, who satisfies your desires with good things so that your youth is renewed like the eagle's.

D *God is Dependable* - to be sure of; reliable; trustworthy

Numbers 23:19 God is not a man, that he should lie, nor a son of man, that he should change his mind. Does he speak and then not act? Does he promise and not fulfill?

E *God is Everlasting* - never coming to an end; lasting forever; eternal

Psalm 90:1-2 Lord, you have been our dwelling place throughout all generations. Before the mountains were born or you brought forth the whole world, from everlasting to everlasting you are God.

F *God is Faithful* - worthy of trust; consistently reliable

Lamentations 3:22-23 Because of the Lord's great love we are not consumed, for his compassions never fail. They are new every morning; great is your faithfulness.

G *God is Good* - honorable, worthy, dependable, reliable, right, thorough, complete, sufficient

Psalm 34:8 Taste and see that the LORD is good; blessed is the man who takes refuge in him.

_____

_____

H *God is Holy* - spiritually perfect or pure; sinless; deserving awe, reverence, adoration

Exodus 15:11 Who among the gods is like you, O LORD? Who is like you -- majestic in holiness, awesome in glory, working wonders?

_____

_____

I *God is Impartial* - favoring no one side or party more than another; without prejudice or bias; fair; just

Psalm 9:7-8 But the Lord reigns forever, executing judgment from His throne. He will judge the world with justice and rule the nations with fairness.

_____

_____

J *God is Just* - conforming to a standard of correctness; righteous

Deuteronomy 32:3-4 I will proclaim the name of the Lord. Oh, praise the greatness of our God! He is the Rock, His works are perfect and all His ways are just. A faithful god who does no wrong, upright and just is He.

_____

_____

K *God is Kind* - sympathetic; friendly; gentle; tenderhearted; generous

Isaiah 63:7 I will tell of the kindnesses of the LORD, the deeds for which he is to be praised, according to all the LORD has done for us - yes, the many good things he has done for the house of Israel, according to his compassion and many kindnesses.

_____

_____

L *God is Love* - strong affection, desire or devotion

Ephesians 3:16-19 I pray that out of his glorious riches, he may strengthen you with power through his Spirit in your inner being, so that Christ may dwell in your hearts through faith. And I pray that you, being rooted and established in love may have power, together with all the saints, to grasp how wide and long and high and deep is the love of Christ, and to know this love that surpasses knowledge that you may be filled to the measure of all the fullness of God.

_____

_____

M *God is Merciful* - forgiving; compassionate

Micah 7:18 Who is a God like you, who pardons sin and forgives the transgression of the remnant of his inheritance? You do not stay angry forever but delight to show mercy.

_____

_____

N *God is Near* - close by

Psalm 145:18 The LORD is near to all who call on him, to all who call on him in truth.

_____

_____

O *God is Omniscient* - having infinite knowledge; knowing all things

Psalm 139:1-6 O LORD, you have searched me and you know me. You know when I sit and when I rise; you perceive my thoughts from afar. You discern my going out and my lying down; you are familiar with all my ways. Before a word is on my tongue you know it completely, O LORD. You hem me in—behind and before; you have laid your hand upon me. Such knowledge is too wonderful for me, too lofty for me to attain.

_____

_____

P *God is Patient* - bearing pains or trials calmly or without complaint; forbearance under provocation or strain

2 Peter 3:9 The Lord is not slow in keeping his promise, as some understand slowness. He is patient with you, not wanting anyone to perish, but everyone to come to repentance.

_____

_____

Q *God is Quick* - rapid; swift

Isaiah 59:9a Then when you call, the LORD will answer. 'Yes, I am here,' he will quickly reply.

_____

_____

R *God is Righteous* - acting in a just, upright manner; doing what is right; morally right; fair and just

Psalm 89:13-15 Your arm is endowed with power; your hand is strong, your right hand exalted. Righteousness and justice are the foundation of your throne; love and faithfulness go before you. Blessed are those who have learned to acclaim you, who walk in the light of your presence, LORD.

_____

_____

S *God is Sovereign* - the most exalted; supreme in excellence and power and authority; unlimited in extent; free from external control

Jeremiah 32:17 Ah, Sovereign LORD, you have made the heavens and the earth by your great power and outstretched arm. Nothing is too hard for you.

_____

_____

T *God is Trustworthy* - dependable; reliable; worthy of placing confidence in, or to put confidently in charge

Psalm 22:4-5 In you our fathers put their trust; they trusted and you delivered them. They cried to you and were saved; in you they trusted and were not disappointed.

_____

_____

U *God is Unfailing* - constant; unflagging (tireless); everlasting; inexhaustible; infallible, sure

Joshua 23:14 Now I am about to go the way of all the earth. You know with all your heart and soul that not one of all the good promises the LORD your God gave you has failed. Every promise has been fulfilled; not one has failed.

_____

_____

V *God is Victorious* - the state of having triumphed; one who overcomes in a battle or struggle

Psalm 44:6-8 I do not trust in my bow, my sword does not bring me victory; but you give us victory over our enemies, you put our adversaries to shame. In God we make our boast all day long and we will praise your name forever.

_____

_____

_____

W *God is Worthy* - intrinsic excellence resulting from superior moral or spiritual qualities; of outstanding worth or importance

Psalm 145:13-21 Your kingdom is an everlasting kingdom, and your dominion endures through all generations. The LORD is faithful to all his promises and loving toward all he has made. The LORD upholds all those who fall and lifts up all who are bowed down. The eyes of all look to you, and you give them their food at the proper time. You open your hand and satisfy the desires of every living thing. The LORD is righteous in all his ways and loving toward all he has made. The LORD is near to all who call on him, to all who call on him in truth. He fulfills the desires of those who fear him; he hears their cry and saves them. The LORD watches over all who love him, but all the wicked he will destroy. My mouth will speak in praise of the LORD. Let every creature praise his holy name for ever and ever.

_____

_____

_____

Whatever your need or concern, whatever difficulty you face, spending time praising God and focusing on who He is brings about a renewed confidence and multiplied faith. By looking at Him first, we see our circumstances through the lens of His character. What may seem difficult or impossible to us can be placed in the hands of the One who created all things. His power is beyond measure. His wisdom is unmatched. God loves us and is able to care for us in ways that we cannot comprehend. Focus on His fullness as we start the journey toward peace.

Which attributes best apply to your life situations? Why?

_____

_____

_____

_____

_____

_____

Praise Exalts God

The Priority of Praise

The Scriptures reveal that God considers praise as a priority. We see this clearly in the first four of the Ten Commandments. God declares that He is God alone and that there is no other. We are instructed that we must not create or worship man made idols. God emphasizes that His name is holy and that we must not misuse it in ways that would dishonor Him. Then He instructs us to set aside a regular time as holy – a time of reverence and adoration - to rest and honor Him.

This is emphasized again in Isaiah 43:10-12(NIV). *"You are my witnesses," declares the Lord, "and my servant whom I have chosen, so that you may know and believe me and understand that I am he. Before me no god was formed, nor will there be one after me. I, even I, am the Lord, and apart from me there is no savior. I have revealed and saved and proclaimed—I, and not some foreign god among you. You are my witnesses," declares the Lord, "that I am God."*

That we were created to bring glory to God is clearly stated in Isaiah 43:7 (NLT) *Bring all who claim me as their God, for I have made them for my glory. It was I who created them.*

God created you and me to bring Him glory. Glory is defined as worshipful adoration or praise. When we glorify God, we exalt and honor Him with extravagant praise. To exalt God means to lift Him up. We exalt God, by recognizing that He is higher than anything else in the universe in terms of greatness and glory.

Exalt God in All Circumstances

Even when we face trials, God quiets our hearts and gives us confidence to exalt Him. This was the situation when David hid in a cave, fleeing from Saul who sought to destroy him.

Read **Psalm 57** List the attributes of God that appear in this passage.

_____

_____

_____

_____

When faced with this threatening situation, what was David's declaration in verses 5 and 11?

_____

_____

Exalting God is more than just speaking words of praise. It is truly believing and acting on the truth that He is God, above all others, sovereign in all situations. It is acknowledging that He loves us deeply and passionately, and has power and might in all our circumstances. It is confessing that He is our everything and that His Word is true. We show this not only by spoken praise, but by living it with conviction.

Another Way to Lift Him Up

In Psalm 99:5 we read, *"Exalt the LORD our God! Bow low before his feet, for he is holy!"* What other way does this verse suggest that we can exalt God?

Not only can we exalt Him by raising our voices in praise – lifting Him up, but also by lowering ourselves – by bowing before Him in humble worship. To bow down, whether physically or within your spirit, is to acknowledge the superiority, the majesty, the holiness of God. The act of bowing before God shows that we yield to Him in respect and in worship. As we bow down, He is lifted up.

All too often, we figuratively "bow" to "things" other than God. By doing so, we are exalting these "things." We are putting them above God, thus disobeying God's commandments. These "things" are usually practical, seemingly necessary "things," but when exalted above God, they are sure to cause distress.

Search me, O God, and know my heart; test me and know my anxious thoughts. Point out anything in me that offends you, and lead me along the path of everlasting life. Psalm 139:23-24 (NLT)

Are there people or things that cause you to bow down? Ask God to reveal anything or anyone that you exalt above Him.

God's commands are designed to guide us in paths leading to peace. When these "things" are placed in the proper priority we are free to focus on God and the many ways He has blessed us. When we exalt God we are filled with joy.

1 Chronicles 16:23-27 (NLT) *Let the whole earth sing to the LORD! Each day proclaim the good news that he saves. Publish his glorious deeds among the nations. Tell everyone about the amazing things he does. Great is the LORD! He is most worthy of praise! He is to be feared above all gods. The gods of other nations are mere idols, but the LORD made the heavens! Honor and majesty surround him; strength and joy fill his dwelling.*

The path to exalting God is one of drawing so near that we know Him intimately. When God draws us near to Himself and we respond, we experience that intimate relationship. When we submit to Him, our faith grows as we experience expressions of His character in our daily lives. Our part is to respond to Him as He reveals His enduring love - to learn about Him and His ways. When we do, the natural outcome is an attitude of gratitude and praise. Our praise exalts God.

All honor and glory to God forever and ever! He is the eternal King, the unseen one who never dies; he alone is God. Amen. 1 Timothy 1:17 (NLT)

Day Four — *Praise Defeats the Enemy*

Stay alert! Watch out for your great enemy, the devil. He prowls around like a roaring lion, looking for someone to devour. 1 Peter 5:8 (NLT)

Let's face it. We have an enemy who is very busy. He attacks in many different ways. He does not rest. Throughout the Scriptures we read accounts of Satan's schemes to bring us down. When we are faced with challenges, all too often we ask the question, "Why?" And just as often that question is followed by a simple two letter word – "me." "Why me?" we ask. And in doing so, the enemy has accomplished his first and most effective blow. He has caused us to focus inward. He has directed our attention to our circumstance and more often than not, our inability to deal with the difficulty. This can lead to a downward spiral than can end in depression, bitterness and despair – right where the enemy wants us.

Not Why? But What?

Because I have experienced this in my own life, I can write about it with authority. That pit of despair, filled with questions, doubts and fears is a lonely place to be. Too often I was unable or unwilling to share my pain, so I "lived with it." It wasn't a good companion. My mind was always occupied with that question.
"Why?"
Over and over the declaration, "I don't understand!" Thoughts turned to tears. Fears resulted in despair. Hope seemed lost. Only recently has the burden been lifted to such an extent that I am amazed.
It was an ordinary day, not unlike the others when I was plagued with questions. In His unique way, God had recently exposed me to two new thoughts.
Yield. Believe.
These thoughts filled my mind with new possibilities.
Hope. Joy.
I had reached a crossroads and had to choose which path I would take. One led to a sad, confusing place. That was not a place where I wanted to dwell. That was not a place where God would take me. That place of accusation, guilt and fear is where the enemy would take me.
God used these new thoughts to put a new question in my mind. "What?" What is it that God wants to teach me? What work is God doing in this situation? This new question led me down a different path. Though I can not see it, or understand it, I know, because of His character, that God is working out things for good. Perhaps that

good is for me, or perhaps it is not about me at all. What ever it might be, I must trust God. I must yield the situation to God. This "yielding" is not a one time event, for the enemy is relentless in his efforts to bring me back into the pit. Now when I sense the doubts arising, it becomes exciting to ask, "What?" It fills me with hope, security and peace. I experience the stretching of my faith as I watch to see how God is working in this situation. I know that in time, His work will become clear and I will see His plan and purpose. And I believe – I know – because it is God at work, I will experience victory. That is the place God wants to take me.

So, I have made a choice. I choose to praise God. I choose to focus on His goodness, His faithfulness, His unfailing love. I choose to praise God. He is victorious. He defeats the enemy. I choose to claim His victory. Today I am filled with anticipation… with hope. Today I choose to ask not "Why?" but "What?" And I wait – expectantly.

Victory through Praise

Earlier in this study we saw how Jesus defeated Satan by responding to the enemy's temptations with God's Word. We identified the points of sin, one of which was pride. Satan was cast out of heaven because of pride. This beautiful creature became corrupted and deceitful, desiring the praise that is worthy of God alone. When we praise God, we acknowledge His greatness and His superiority over Satan. When we put our trust in Him and declare that He is victorious, the enemy is defeated.

In 2 Chronicles 20:6-22 we find an incredible account where praise defeated the enemy. The nation of Judah led by King Jehoshsphat was surrounded by several armies of enemies ready for war. Jehoshaphat was terrified. Although he was not as faithful to trust God in smaller matters, Jehoshaphat knew that God was his only hope in this, a battle for survival. He stands before his people and prays to God.

Read **2 Chronicles 20: 6-12** How does Jehoshaphat address God in verse 6?

_____

_____

What does he ask of God in verse 12? _____

_____

As the people stand waiting, God speaks through Jahaziel, one of the men in the crowd.

Read verses 15-17 What does he tell them at the end of verse 15?

_____

_____

What are their instructions in verse 17? _____

_____

What did Jehoshaphat and all the people do in verses 18-19? _____

_____

_____

In verse 20, what words of instruction and encouragement did Jehoshaphat give to his people?

_____

_____

Read verses 21-22 What was the turning point of the battle? _____

_____

_____

Read verse 24

When the army of Judah arrived, ready to enter the battle, what did they find?_____

_____

_____

What was the weapon that defeated the enemy? _____

_____

_____

As you read the following scriptures, underline the attributes of God. Consider how praise defeats the enemy.

2 Samuel 22:3-4 (NLT) My God is my rock, in whom I find protection. He is my shield, the power that saves me, and my place of safety. He is my refuge, my savior, the one who saves me from violence. I called on the LORD, who is worthy of praise, and he saved me from my enemies.

Psalm 18:1-3 (NLT) A psalm of David, the servant of the Lord. He sang this song to the Lord on the day the Lord rescued him from all his enemies and from Saul. He sang: I love you, LORD; you are my strength. The LORD is my rock, my fortress, and my savior; my God is my rock, in whom I find protection. He is my shield, the power that saves me, and my place of safety. I called on the LORD, who is worthy of praise, and he saved me from my enemies.

Isaiah 33:21-22 (NLT) The LORD will be our Mighty One. He will be like a wide river of protection that no enemy can cross, that no enemy ship can sail upon. For the LORD is our judge, our lawgiver, and our king. He will care for us and save us.

Psalm 62:5-8 (NLT) Let all that I am wait quietly before God, for my hope is in him. He alone is my rock and my salvation, my fortress where I will not be shaken. My victory and honor come from God alone. He is my refuge, a rock where no enemy can reach me. O my people, trust in him at all times. Pour out your heart to him, for God is our refuge.

Fill your day with praise and the enemy is defeated. Transform your attitude from "Why me?" to "You, Lord God, are victorious."

Praise Changes You

The Day I Will Never Forget

Are there specific days that stand out in your memory? Birthdays, graduations and weddings often make the list. But the event that remains a vivid picture in my mind happened on an ordinary day as I drove to work. For several years before this day I met weekly with a group of mothers to pray for our children. My prayer life had changed through these years as I learned a new way to pray. Before bringing our requests to God in prayer we took time to focus totally on God and praise Him. After several years praying with these moms I began to discover that focusing on God's character brought about more confidence as I prayed. I was learning more about who God is through studying His attributes in the scriptures. These experiences were the background that led to a day when my life took a dramatic turn.

My younger daughter, Laura, would soon be a junior in high school and had struggled with math throughout her school years. The teachers, the counselor and I agreed that my daughter would do best if she learned math one on one. Using a correspondence course for Algebra II, I became her teacher. I was willing but my student was a bit reluctant.

So, from September to May, we struggled, we plodded, she worked every problem with me hanging over her shoulder, encouraging, explaining, forcing the way through the course. We would spend time in each session negotiating how much time she must study the lesson and how many problems she had to work. It felt like walking through mud with a ball and chain – for both of us! Although she had worked every problem and turned in all the assignments, the final grade was determined only by the grade on the final exam. If she failed this final test, she failed the course. We reviewed and reworked as much as she could bear and she left for school that morning to take the test.

I remember driving by the school on my way to work that morning, praying – pleading with God to help her remember, to help her read the questions clearly, to understand each problem, to work the problems correctly. As I was tearfully pleading with God – He spoke to my heart very clearly. "Carol, don't focus on what Laura can do, focus on what I can do." It was at that moment that all of those attributes I had prayed came flooding through my mind – God is faithful – God is able – God is wisdom and knowledge – God is victorious – God cares and on and on. As I began to shift my focus from Laura's abilities to the character of God, the burden was lifted and replaced with peace. I was assured as I focused on the fact that God is good; God is sovereign. I knew that God was in control. I began to praise God and put my hope in Him. As I did, I experienced an overwhelming peace and joy that spilled out in continuous praise. Even without knowing what the outcome of the test would be, I was at peace. I shared this with my daughter and together we trusted in God. When we got the results, Laura had made an A on the test.

In that life changing moment God revealed Himself to me in a clear way. As I learn more and more about His character, my heart is filled with praise. Praising God has become the foundation of a growing faith and trust in Him. Now, when I face challenges or difficulties, rather than focusing on the problem or focusing on how I can solve it, I shift my focus to God and praise Him for who He is. As I am focused on the One who understands, the One who can meet my every need, I take a giant step in the journey to peace.

Praise Transforms You

God tells us in Romans 12:2 (NLT) *Don't copy the behavior and customs of this world, but let God transform you into a new person by changing the way you think. Then you will learn to know God's will for you, which is good and pleasing and perfect.*

Once again, we must consider the enemy. This verse says that God will transform us by changing the way we _____. When our thinking has been transformed, we will be able to know God's _____ for our life. We will also know that His will for us is _____ and _____ and _____.

To think that the enemy will give in and allow this transformation to be simple is to underestimate him. Why would the enemy fight this transformation? Until our thinking is transformed, we are back to the "Why me?" state of mind. This transformation is an ongoing process as we journey through life. We must choose to live in God's truth and become keenly aware of the half lies of Satan that masquerade as truth. As we continually renew our minds, we begin to know and understand God's perfect plan for our lives.

Read **James 4:7** God's word states that if we _____ the enemy he will _____. As we studied earlier, the power to resist the enemy rests in focusing on God and _____ Him.

The Greatest Commandment

In Matthew 22:36-38 (NLT), Jesus is questioned by the religious leaders who are trying to test his knowledge of the law. They ask, *"Teacher, which is the most important commandment in the law of Moses?" Jesus replied, "'You must love the LORD your God with all your heart, all your soul, and all your mind.' This is the first and greatest commandment."*

Why would this be considered the greatest commandment? God wants us to know Him, heart soul and mind. He wants us to know His character and to know that nothing will ever change His great love for us. As we follow this commandment, we discover that He truly is amazing. He wants us to know that He plans good things for us and that His plan for our future is a hopeful one. Grasping this truth within our spirit is life changing. When we begin to comprehend the depth of His love, we will praise Him more perfectly and grow to know Him even more intimately. Praise is the root of all joy and the joy comes as a result of being in God's presence. The more we know Him, the greater our joy.

Don't Waste the Seeds

Jesus taught the parable of the four soils to illustrate different responses to God's message. The four conditions of the soil represented its readiness to receive the seed.

Read **Matthew 13:3-9**

List the four conditions of soil in which the seeds were scattered.

1) _____

2) _____

3) _____

4) _____

Read **Matthew 13:18-23**

Jesus explains the parable and applies it to those who hear God's message. List what happened to the seeds in each of the four types of soil.

1) _____

2) _____

3) _____

4) _____

In three of the four types of soil, the seeds were wasted – never producing fruit.

All too often I have found myself "wasting the seeds." There are times when I hear a wonderful message, enjoy the fellowship of believers, comment on how well it applies to my life, then as I walk out the door the enemy shows up and I let him steal my joy. Other times I become so busy that I forget the message and continue down the familiar path I have always walked, sidestepping the joy. When I allow worries and troubles to occupy my mind, I crowd out the joy and my heart is heavy. The seeds of God's Word are wasted because I have not cultivated my heart in a way that they will produce fruit.

The past few days we have been studying praise. We have examined the scriptures and answered the question, "Why Praise?" We have focused on several of the attributes of God's character that illustrate how worthy He is of our praise and how we exalt God when we praise Him. The scriptures have revealed how praising God defeats the enemy. But if all we do is consider the truth of what we have studied and not put it into practice, we are merely "wasting the seeds." There will be no fruit – no change that will lead us to the peace that is the destination of our journey. The key to progress on our journey is to practice praise. When we do, it becomes a natural part of our day and we find God's goodness surrounding us, inspiring constant praise as we acknowledge the ways He is at work in our daily lives. The journey becomes hopeful and joyful as we make praise a priority. It is not a task, but a privilege to welcome God into every part of our day through praise.

Practice Praise

Go back to the attributes and speak them out loud. Rather than saying, "God is

_____" say, "God, You are _____ and I praise You!" Take time to lavish Him with praise and experience the change that praise brings. Some have said that God inhabits praise. I believe it is true, for when we praise Him, His presence becomes very real. Practice praise. Make that choice throughout the day and an awareness of God's presence will lead you to worship. It will propel you forward on the journey to peace.

And now, dear brothers and sisters, one final thing. Fix your thoughts on what is true, and honorable, and right, and pure, and lovely, and admirable. Think about things that are excellent and worthy of praise. Keep putting into practice all you learned and received from me—everything you heard from me and saw me doing. Then the God of peace will be with you. Philippians 4:8-9(NLT)

Clearing the Way

Repent

There are times when we find ourselves headed the wrong way on our journey to peace. When we acknowledge our mistake and turn around, we can continue the journey. Now we will look at the process of getting back on the right road.

Obstacles

One of the biggest obstacles we will face as we travel on the journey to peace is sin. Satan's main goal is to cause us to turn away from God. What could cause us to turn away? The enemy knows that when we stand in the presence of God free from sin, we are filled with peace and joy. But just as it did when Adam and Eve sinned by disobeying God, sin causes us to avoid being in God's presence. The truth is that all of our sins have been covered at the cross. Yet the enemy is relentless as he tries to steal our peace. As we learned in week one day five, there are three points from which all sin originates. What are those three points?

1) _____

2) _____

3) _____

Temptation

Satan uses these three points to tempt us, just as he did Jesus. The temptations arising from these three points come in many ways. List some temptations from each point of sin that the enemy might use to draw us away from God.

1) _____

2) _____

3) _____

Distractions

When we are tempted, we are offered something that tries to persuade or entice us to engage in behaviors that will shift our focus away from God. We become distracted. The temptation allures us with such a seductive pull that we easily lose our focus. The purpose of temptation is to distract us from focusing on the fullness of God. What Satan offers is often a counterfeit of the peace and joy that we experience when we are focused on God.

What are some of the things that distract you from focusing on your relationship with God?

_____

_____

_____

_____

Maintaining Focus

In the 2011 NBA finals, the Dallas Mavericks were facing the Miami Heat. With a trio of what some considered the best players in the league led by LeBron James, commonly referred to as "King James," the Miami Heat were favored to win. King James was intimidating with his abilities as an athlete, however, as the series progressed, it seemed that he was not living up to his reputation, especially in the final periods of the games. Guarding this giant athlete was a much smaller player, Jason Terry. When the cameras zoomed in on the pair, often it appeared that Jason Terry was always talking and it became evident that this constant chatter, sometimes called "trash talk" was having an impact on the performance of King James. When asked about this, Jason Terry replied, "Why do I trash talk? I trash talk to distract him, because if he gets focused, I can't stop him."

In the same way, if we keep focused on God and avoid the distractions, the enemy is powerless. The enemy knows that if we are focused on the fullness of God, the temptations he offers can be overcome.

The Blame Game

There was a comedian who was widely known for a famous quote. When behaving badly in his comedy skits, he often turned to the audience and innocently said, "The devil made me do it!" Although the devil throws temptations in our path, we cannot blame him when we give in and do wrong. We alone are responsible for our choices. And we do have a choice. We can give in to the temptation, which is sin, or we can ask God to help by giving us the strength and inner courage to turn away.

Help from God's Word

A verse I memorized early in my walk of faith is one I highly recommend that you memorize. It is a powerful weapon when faced with temptation.

1 Corinthians 10:13 (NLT) *The temptations in your life are no different from what others experience. And God is faithful. He will not allow the temptation to be more than you can stand. When you are tempted, he will show you a way out so that you can endure.*

Write out this verse in your own words.

_____

_____

_____

_____

_____

Remember, we are "all in the same boat." We are all faced with temptations, but on the other hand, we all can trust God to help us resist the temptation, for He has overcome the power of sin.

Read **James 1:12-14**

What does God promise to those who resist temptation? _____

_____

Does temptation ever come from God? _____

According to verse 14, what is the root of temptation that Satan uses so effectively?

_____

_____

Although with God's help we can resist temptation, often we fall prey to our desires. Sin becomes a big roadblock on our journey to peace. How can we clear the way? Once again, God has the answer. The next session will explore the process of removing the obstacles that block the way on the journey to peace.

Confession Day Two

Romans 3:23 (NLT) *For everyone has sinned; we all fall short of God's glorious standard.*

In Romans 7:18-19(NLT), the Apostle Paul describes what we all experience at one time or another. He writes, *"And I know that nothing good lives in me, that is, in my sinful nature. I want to do what is right, but I can't. I want to do what is good, but I don't. I don't want to do what is wrong, but I do it anyway."*

Perhaps you can identify with Paul's words. We must realize however that, although we are subject to sin because of our sin nature, we are not bound by sin because Jesus Christ has conquered sin. If we look to Him for help, we will not have to give in to sin. We should never live with the excuse that "the devil made me do it." We must assume responsibility when we choose to yield to temptation.

Why Confess?

When temptation results in sin, the road to peace is blocked. The one way to remove the roadblock is to confess the sin and assume responsibility for our disobedience to God. When we confess, we admit or acknowledge guilt or fault. The enemy would have us believe that we can hide our sin. Pride, one of the points of sin, raises its head and we feel empowered thinking that no one will ever know about our sin. There are times when we are able to hide our sins from those around us, but there is no sin that is hidden from God. He not only sees our acts, but He knows our heart. When we confess our sin, we are simply agreeing with what God already knows.

Sin causes us to avoid God. It even causes us to doubt the truth that God will never leave us or forsake us. The enemy accuses us that we have not been faithful and that we have failed. Because of our sin we feel unworthy to approach God. As the following verse demonstrates, the burden of sin is heavy and results in despair.

Psalm 51:9-11 (NLT) *Don't keep looking at my sins. Remove the stain of my guilt. Create in me a clean heart, O God. Renew a loyal spirit within me. Do not banish me from your presence, and don't take your Holy Spirit from me.*

Clearing the Roadblock

Unconfessed sin is a heavy burden. Some sins become so ingrained in our lives that we resist acknowledging them as sin. We feel that we cannot live without the burden, even though it weighs us down. We must not be afraid to allow the Holy Spirit to reveal our sin. When sin is revealed, we must choose whether we will acknowledge it or bury it with distractions.

In order to continue on the journey to peace, we must clear away the roadblocks. Now is the time to take care of the necessary business that will prevent further delay on our journey.

Read **Psalm 139:23-24** Pray and ask God to reveal sin in your life, past or present. Humble yourself and take time to hear the Holy Spirit. Confess – agree with God when sin is revealed and ask forgiveness.

When the Burden is Lifted

Confession frees us from the burden of sin. According to the following scripture, it wipes the record of sin clean.

Read **1 John 1:9** and write it below.

_____

_____

_____

_____

According to this verse, to what degree are your sins forgiven?

_____

What separates us from God is denying our sin due to pride. You will not surprise God with your confession. It will release the burden of sin and break down the wall that separates you from the peace that comes from God alone. Always remember, when it comes to sin, the enemy accuses – God forgives.

Benefits of Confession

In the scriptures that follow we see the joy, peace and relief that results from confessing our sin. Read each verse and list the benefits of confessing sin.

Proverbs 28:13 People who conceal their sins will not prosper, but if they confess and turn from them, they will receive mercy.

_____

_____

Psalm 66:17-19 For I cried out to him for help, praising him as I spoke. If I had not confessed the sin in my heart, the Lord would not have listened. But God did listen! He paid attention to my prayer.

_____

_____

Psalm 32:2-6 Yes, what joy for those whose record the LORD has cleared of guilt, whose lives are lived in complete honesty! When I refused to confess my sin, my body wasted away, and I groaned all day long. Day and night your hand of discipline was heavy on me. My strength evaporated like water in the summer heat. Finally, I confessed all my sins to you and stopped trying to hide my guilt. I said to myself, "I will confess my rebellion to the LORD." And you forgave me! All my guilt is gone.

_____

_____

_____

Forgiveness

Psalm 51:7 (NLT) _Purify me from my sins, and I will be clean; wash me, and I will be whiter than snow._

Forgiveness may seem simple. A sincere confession and our sin is gone. Though simple for us, our forgiveness came at great cost.

Consider the Cost

In the Old Testament specific instructions were given in the law that must be followed to receive forgiveness for sin. The following passage reveals how difficult it would be to keep the law perfectly in order to receive forgiveness.

Leviticus 4:27-31 *If a member of the community sins unintentionally and does what is forbidden in any of the LORD's commands, he is guilty. When he is made aware of the sin he committed, he must bring as his offering for the sin he committed a female goat without defect. He is to lay his hand on the head of the sin offering and slaughter it at the place of the burnt offering. Then the priest is to take some of the blood with his finger and put it on the horns of the altar of burnt offering and pour out the rest of the blood at the base of the altar. He shall remove all the fat, just as the fat is removed from the fellowship offering, and the priest shall burn it on the altar as an aroma pleasing to the LORD. In this way the priest will make atonement for him, and he will be forgiven.*

Read **Hebrews 10:1-18** and answer these questions.

In verse 1, the Old Testament law is referred to as a _____ of things

to come. How effective were these sacrifices in the cleansing of sin? _____

_____

In verse 2, what evidence shows that these sacrifices were not adequate to permanently

bring about forgiveness? _____

_____

In verses 3-4, other than forgiveness, what purpose did the sacrifices accomplish? ___

_____

According to verse 5, who spoke the following words? *"You did not want animal sacrifices or sin offerings. But you have given me a body to offer. You were not pleased with burnt offerings or other offerings for sin. Then I said, 'Look, I have come to do your will, O God—as is written about me in the Scriptures.'"*

_____

Write out verse 10. _____

_____

_____

According to verse 14, this one sacrifice has made us _____

_____

What does verse 17, say about our sins? _____

_____

Read verse 18. What does this imply about the Old Testament sacrifice compared to the sacrifice of Jesus Christ? _____

_____

The feeling of relief and freedom, knowing that God forgives and forgets our sin is expressed in Romans 4:7-8 (NLT) *Oh, what joy for those whose disobedience is forgiven, whose sins are put out of sight. Yes, what joy for those whose record the LORD has cleared of sin.*

When Sin Seems Too Great

It is hard to comprehend how a Holy God can forgive and forget our sin as a result of a simple, yet sincere confession. Our guilt overwhelms us and we find it hard to confess. Sometimes it almost seems easier to feel guilty than to ask forgiveness. This was shown to me so clearly one day when my granddaughter was visiting. I don't remember the transgression, but I took her aside and tried to help her understand that she needed to ask forgiveness. Tearfully sobbing and in agony, knowing that she had done something wrong, she cried out, "I can't say I'm sorry! I can't! It's too hard."

There are times when we feel that our sin is so great that we cannot approach God to ask forgiveness. The enemy skillfully accuses and convinces us that we can never be washed clean. Once again, pride gets in the way. Yet there is no sin so great, that the blood of Jesus is not sufficient to wash our soul clean. We must only be obedient to humble ourselves and confess it to Him. Then we must accept the forgiveness that He freely offers. When forgiven, we must choose to take off the cloak of guilt that the enemy would have us wear and rejoice in the newness of life that we receive. The result is healing and an overwhelming love and gratitude to the One who forgives.

If you, O LORD, kept a record of sins, O Lord, who could stand? But with you there is forgiveness; therefore you are feared. I wait for the LORD, my soul waits, and in his word I put my hope. Psalm 130:3-5

The Greater Cost

Although the physical sacrifice can be somewhat understood, I wonder if it is possible to comprehend the true nature of the sacrifice that frees us from our sin. In order to begin to understand how completely God loves us, we must realize that God, the creator of the universe, King of King, Lord of Lords, the one true God was willing to humble himself, take on human flesh, live a simple life, physically suffer and die to pay the price for our sin.

The fact that we must only confess our sin seems so very simple in comparison. When we begin to see the depth of what God did to redeem us from sin, we begin to see how great was the cost.

Surely he took up our pain and bore our suffering, yet we considered him punished by God, stricken by him, and afflicted. But he was pierced for our transgressions, he was crushed for our iniquities; the punishment that brought us peace was on him, and by his wounds we are healed. Isaiah 53:4-5

Brokenness

When we face our sin and consider the sacrifice that God suffered in order to offer forgiveness, we are able to break through the fleshly desires and pride and come to a place of brokenness where God is able to minister to our spirit.

Repeat Offenders

There is a worship song with the lyric, "My chains are gone. I've been set free." While singing this song, I visualized a prisoner being released from prison. But then, as I thought about those freed prisoners, I realized that all too often, they become repeat offenders and find themselves back in prison.

I must confess I, too, am a repeat offender. Even though I experience freedom when I confess my sin, all too often when confronted with the same temptations, I yield to my human desires. Perhaps I am not alone. Before I will turn from my sin completely, I must be broken. I must realize that alone I am powerless over sin. I must acknowledge how much I need to trust in the power of Jesus Christ to free me from my sin. Only then are the chains forever gone. Only then am I truly free.

The Purpose of Brokenness

In the book of Job, we read the account of a man who is wealthy and respected. He is healthy, has a large family and a lives a comfortable lifestyle. Suddenly, and seemingly without cause, Job loses everything – his health, his family, his possessions and his friends. Read Job 17 to see a picture of one who is broken.

Although Job did not understand why God allowed such suffering, he endured because his life was built upon faith in God. Job discovered at his lowest point that God alone was enough. When all else is stripped away, we can see God more clearly. In Job 42:5, Job speaks these words: *My ears had heard of you but now my eyes have seen you. Therefore I despise myself and repent in dust and ashes."*

Brokenness allows us to see the greatness of God and leads to repentance.

Brokenness Changes our Perspective

God allows brokenness to bring us to a place where we no longer trust in ourselves, but trust in God. At times we are like stubborn mules that cannot be broken. This is illustrated in Psalm 32:8-9 (NLT) *The LORD says, "I will guide you along the best pathway for your life. I will advise you and watch over you. Do not be like a senseless horse or mule that needs a bit and bridle to keep it under control."*

The human nature of mankind says, "I can do it myself. I don't need help." It is beyond reason to understand why we would not submit to God, creator and sustainer of the universe who, as the verse says "will guide us along the best pathway." Yet over and over, we stubbornly resist, only to find ourselves defeated and damaged. Without

God, we cannot be whole. But God uses brokenness to draw us to himself. It is not until we are broken that we can admit that we are powerless over sin. Adam and Eve were so wounded by their sin of disobedience that they hid from God. They ran away from the One who could heal their brokenness. We must come into His presence free from judgment and self righteousness but acknowledging that we are broken. Brokenness allows us to realize that He alone is able to heal us and to make us whole again.

When we acknowledge our brokenness, we approach God with a humble heart, depending on Him alone. We are changed as we focus on God and yield to His control. We are able to focus on the needs of others and yield our thoughts, our tongue and our actions to be used in building the Kingdom of God.

God Wounds but also Heals

Psalm 51:17 (NLT) *The sacrifice you desire is a broken spirit. You will not reject a broken and repentant heart, O God.*

According to this verse, what is the benefit of a broken repentant heart?

_____

_____

When my husband severely broke both bones in his lower leg, the doctor said the bones in the x-ray looked like a bunch of jumbled puzzle pieces. There were complications and infections over a period of four years that required several surgeries to try to heal the bones. Each time they operated, they had to make wounds on his leg so that the infection could be cleaned out and for the bones to be secured with hardware. The last thing they did after each surgery was to carefully bandage the wounds they had caused so that his leg could heal. It was some time later that I read the following verse: Job 5:17-19 (NLT) *But consider the joy of those corrected by God! Do not despise the discipline of the Almighty when you sin. For though he wounds, he also bandages. He strikes, but his hands also heal.*

I had never considered that God causes wounds. After reading this verse, because of the experience we had gone through with my husband's broken leg, I realized that, just as the surgeons did, God only causes wounds that will bring about healing. The wounds we suffer at His hand, He will bandage with His love and heal with His forgiveness. When we are healed, we are whole, new and better than before.

The book of Job ends telling that God restored Job's health, his wealth and his family with twice as much as he had before. The greatest blessing, however, was that through the testing of his faith, Job had seen and experienced the faithfulness of God as never before.

Read **Psalm 34:18** and write it on the lines below.

_____

_____

_____

God does not abandon those who are broken. He comes to their rescue.

Are You Broken?

What does it require for one to become broken? Is it something that is forced on us externally? Is it a choice? Jesus shows us the example of brokenness in Philippians 2:5-8 (NLT) *You must have the same attitude that Christ Jesus had. Though he was God, he did not think of equality with God as something to cling to. Instead, he gave up his divine privileges; he took the humble position of a slave and was born as a human being. When he appeared in human form, he humbled himself in obedience to God and died a criminal's death on a cross.*

Was this an easy thing for Jesus to do? Did it require brokenness?
Read **Matthew 26: 36-44**
In this account we see the struggle that Jesus experienced as he faced the cross. What words did He say in verse 38 that describe the extent of his struggle?

_____

How many times did he plead with God to be delivered from the suffering he would

soon face? _____

Have you come to a point of brokenness? If so, what did God reveal to you that

could only come as a result of brokenness? _____

_____

_____

_____

_____

He heals the brokenhearted and bandages their wounds. Psalm 147:3

Day Five — Repent

The past four days of study have prepared us to take the second step to peace. We have examined how temptation can lead to sin and how confession of our sin brings forgiveness. We have considered how understanding the price paid for our sin can lead to brokenness. But if we desire to take another step in the journey to peace, we must repent. The heaviness of our sin as revealed by the Holy Spirit must weigh so greatly that it brings about sorrow and regret. The regret coupled with the desire to have nothing that bars us from our relationship with God should result in a change of mind and a change of behavior. Considering the cost of our human desires that cause us to walk away from God, we must turn away from our sin and turn toward God. Repentance frees us from sin so that it no longer holds power over us, enslaving us to a life of guilt and shame. Freed from the obstacles of sin, we can take a second step toward peace.

A Change of Mind

Romans 12:2a (NIV) *Do not conform to the pattern of this world, but be transformed by the renewing of your mind.*

A change in how we live begins with a "renewing" or change in our mind. When this change in how we think becomes seated in our heart, with God's power, we change how we live.

We repent.

Repentance is Action

The picture of repentance is an action picture. It is a picture of walking toward darkness, then turning around completely and walking toward light.

Read **Acts 26:18**

In this verse, Paul is giving an account of his encounter with Jesus on the road to Damascus. It states that Paul's mission from God is to help people turn from _____

_____ to _____ and from the power of

to _____.

This action of turning around and heading in the opposite direction starts by changing how we look at things. What might seem acceptable in light of today's society might be viewed differently if we view it from God's point of view. When this change in how we think becomes seated in our heart, with God's power we can change how we act and how we live.

Ephesians 5:8-10 (NLT) gives us words of guidance. *For once you were full of darkness, but now you have light from the Lord. So live as people of light! For this light within you produces only what is good and right and true. Carefully determine what pleases the Lord.*

Examples from Scripture

In the scriptures we find several passages that teach about repentance. In 2 Samuel 12, we read the account of Nathan the prophet who God used to confront King David after he had committed adultery with Bathsheba and arranged for her husband's death. Realizing his sin, David confessed and repented. Read **Psalm 51:1-17**.

This passage of scripture illustrates how sin wounds the soul of man. In verses 1-5, what words or phrases illustrate the condemnation that sin brings?

_____

_____

_____

_____

In verse 6 we see a transition take place. David's focus shifts from confessing his sin. What becomes his focus starting in this verse? _____

_____

In verses 7-11 what does David ask of God? _____

_____

_____

_____

Verses 12-13 suggest that David wants God to use him in what way? _____

_____

In verses 14-15 what does David suggest will be the result of God's forgiveness? _____

_____

In verses 16-17 it appears that David understands that God's grace supersedes the Law. What does David say that shows this? _____

_____

_____

How would David know this? In 1 Samuel 13:14, when Samuel tells King Saul that he will no longer be King, he refers to the person who God has chosen to replace him as "a man after his own heart." That man was David – a man who knew the heart of God.

Practice Repentance

Although sin may enter our lives at times, if we truly are repentant, we will not allow sin to become a welcome companion.

Read **1 John 3:9** and **1 John 5:18**

Both verses state that those who are God's children do not _____ sinning.

To practice sin, according to the dictionary, would be "to do or engage in frequently or usually" – literally to make sin a habit. Behaviors that come easily, that can be done often without even thinking are habits. Sin can disguise itself as a simple habit. Unless we yield our thoughts actions and attitudes to God on a moment by moment basis, it is possible – even probable – that we are engaging in sin. Although we might be tempted to excuse our sinful behavior as minor, there is no scale that measures the severity of sin. It is simple – sin is sin. Even the smallest sin was great enough to require the sacrifice that Jesus paid on the cross so that our sins might be forgiven.

It was not until I began to understand what it means to truly repent that I became convicted of daily sin. Although I did not rob a bank or engage in illegal activities, my spirit became keenly aware of my sinful attitudes and thoughts. I was amazed at how judgmental I had become. Ugly attitudes began to surface and sins of unforgiveness were revealed. As I asked God to reveal my sin, the Holy Spirit quickly spoke to my heart when I sinned. I found it much easier to immediately confess my sin, receive forgiveness, turn away from sin and turn to God. I began to practice repentance.

It is amazing how often we realize that sin pops up in everyday life when we become in tune with the Holy Spirit. Before God taught me how to "practice repentance," at the end of the day I would simply pray, "forgive me of my sins." All too often I would think to myself, "I can't think of any sin I need to confess at the moment, but I'll ask forgiveness because I know that is what I should do." How can we repent and turn away from sin if we don't know what sin we are turning from? How can we turn away unless we become aware of steps we are taking toward sin? Only as our sin is revealed can we immediately choose to repent and walk the other way. Only as we "tune in" to the Holy Spirit will we become aware of our sin.

The enemy would have us believe that we seldom commit sin that calls for repentance. The truth is found in 1 John 5:21 (NLT) *Dear children, keep away from anything that might take God's place in your hearts.* Using this as a gauge for sin, our guilt is revealed.

Repent and Experience Freedom

As we repent and turn away from sin, we see that what we turn to is an incredible gift. We turn to forgiveness. We turn to grace. We turn to freedom. We turn to hope. We turn to Jesus, our Lord and Savior.

Romans 6:12-14 The Message reminds us that repentance is a moment by moment choice. *That means you must not give sin a vote in the way you conduct your lives. Don't give it the time of day. Don't even run little errands that are connected with that old way of life. Throw yourselves wholeheartedly and full-time—remember, you've been raised from the dead!—into God's way of doing things. Sin can't tell you how to live. After all, you're not living under that old tyranny any longer. You're living in the freedom of God.*

The only place we find true freedom and true significance is in God. Sin keeps us away from God. Repentance brings us back to Him and takes us one step closer to peace.

Week Four

Stop and Smell the Roses
Acknowledge

We have just taken a difficult step in our journey, but one that results in freedom. We now can enjoy fellowship with God and freedom from sin as we continue on the journey to peace. This next step is one that will bring joy as we clear away the distractions and focus on the blessings we experience moment by moment. Our lives can become so busy that we overlook the beauty of each day. This step requires that we stop and smell the roses as we continue our journey.

Day One — Blessings

Our lives are filled with one blessing after another every moment of every day. Before you take exception to this statement, let us explore the concept of blessings.

"Blessing" is defined as anything that gives happiness or prevents misfortune. It is commonly considered to be a special benefit or favor. All too often I have overlooked the many blessings that are a part of my everyday life. Consider just a few.

Life. The gift that God has spoken into being and breathed into mankind.

Water. An incredible combination of hydrogen and oxygen molecules that flow in a cycle that fills the oceans and waters the earth.

The Human Body and its perfect design with the ability to heal itself.

Seeds that in the presence of dirt, water and air burst into plants that produce delicious fruits, vegetables and grains.

On and on the list could go filled with all the wonders of creation. Yet that would only begin to tell the story of God's many benefits.

Read Psalm **103:1-5** List the "benefits" that are mentioned in this passage.

_____

_____

_____

_____

Do we recognize these blessings or are we looking for something else? Perhaps we are looking for material things that will fulfill our human desires. God's blessings have a much more permanent purpose. His blessings are designed to benefit our lives in more meaningful ways.

Blessings from God's Word

The scriptures are filled with God's promise of blessing. Though we may be undeserving, it is apparent that God wants to bless His children. Some blessings are conditional, but the conditions are always given to direct us in ways that are beneficial and result in blessing. God's blessings are given so that we may in turn bless others. His blessings are passed on from one generation to another if we continue to trust in Him and seek His will.

Read the following scripture and underline all the ways that God promises to bless. Deuteronomy 28:2-8 (NLT) *You will experience all these blessings IF you obey the Lord your God: You will be blessed in your towns and in the country. You will be blessed with many children and productive fields. You will be blessed with fertile herds and flocks. You will be blessed with baskets overflowing with fruit, and with kneading bowls filled with bread. You will be blessed wherever you go, both in coming and in going. The Lord will conquer your enemies when they attack you... And the Lord will bless everything you do and will fill your storehouses with grain.*

What is the condition required for these blessings?

_____

Although there are many blessings we experience from the gift of life itself, there are many more blessings that we are promised if we are obedient to God.

Read the following scriptures:

Psalm 1:1-3 What is the promise given in this verse to those who delight in the law of God? _____

Psalm 112:1-2 According to this verse who also benefits when we obey God's commands?

_____

James 1:12 When we face trials, if we love God, what are we promised to receive?

_____

The Beatitudes

Matthew 5:3-11 (NLT) is part of what is referred to as the Sermon on the Mount. Jesus had become well known and everyone wanted to see Him. The disciples were those closest to Jesus and may have enjoyed the prestige that came from being associated with Him. As the crowds gathered, Jesus began speaking with words that seemed to contradict each other. Often referred to as The Beatitudes, this part of His sermon helps us understand that the blessings of God are often quite different from the blessings the world has to offer.

God blesses those who are poor and realize their need for him, for the Kingdom of Heaven is theirs. God blesses those who mourn, for they will be comforted. God blesses those who are humble, for they will inherit the whole earth. God blesses those who hunger and thirst for justice, for they will be satisfied. God blesses those who are merciful, for they will be shown mercy. God blesses those whose hearts are pure, for they will see God. God blesses those who work for peace, for they will be called the children of God. God blesses those who are persecuted for doing right, for the Kingdom of Heaven is theirs. God blesses you when people mock you and persecute you and lie about you and say all sorts of evil things against you because you are my followers.

True blessing comes from knowing, trusting and serving God. Read **Jeremiah 17:7** and write it out below.

_____

_____

_____

_____

_____

Read and receive this beautiful blessing from God's Word.

May the LORD bless you and protect you. May the LORD smile on you and be gracious to you. May the LORD show you his favor and give you his peace. Numbers 6:24-26 (NLT)

Day Two — *God's Character*

To further understand true blessings, we will spend two days studying the character of God as revealed in scripture

God's Work Reveals His Character

Just as we praise God for who He is, we thank God for what He does. All that God does is a reflection of His character. The foundation of all that He does is His unconditional, unfailing love. In the next two days we will read scriptures that show how God's character is revealed through His work in our daily lives. Each action represents a way that God works in our lives.

Read the definition of each action and consider how God's work is an expression of His love. Then read the scriptures and take time to consider how God has acted in your behalf or in the lives of others. Write expressions of thanksgiving for each characteristic describing the ways you have seen Him working in your life.

God Builds

Build: to make by putting together; to order, plan or direct the construction of; to cause to be or grow; create; develop

Acts 20:32 (NLT) And now I entrust you to God and the message of his grace that is able to build you up and give you an inheritance with all those he has set apart for himself.

_____

_____

_____

God Cares

Care: close attention or careful heed; to feel concern or interest in

1 Peter 5:7 (NLT) Give all your worries and cares to God, for he cares about you.

_____

_____

_____

God Comforts

Comfort: to encourage, help and strengthen; to console, calm or inspire with hope

2 Thessalonians 2:16-17 (NLT) Now may our Lord Jesus Christ himself and God our Father, who loved us and by his grace gave us eternal comfort and a wonderful hope, comfort you and strengthen you in every good thing you do and say.

_____

_____

_____

God Corrects

Correct: to set right with remedies, revisions, or reforms

Job 5:17 (NLT) But consider the joy of those corrected by God! Do not despise the discipline of the Almighty when you sin.

_____

_____

_____

God Calms our Fears

Fear: a feeling of anxiety, uneasiness or apprehension by the presence or nearness of danger, evil, or pain.

Isaiah 41:10 (NLT) Don't be afraid, for I am with you. Don't be discouraged, for I am your God. I will strengthen you and help you. I will hold you up with my victorious right hand.

_____

_____

_____

God Finishes

Finish: to bring to an end; to complete; to give final touches to, embellish or perfect

Philippians 1:6 (NLT) And I am certain that God, who began the good work within you, will continue his work until it is finally finished on the day when Christ Jesus returns.

_____

_____

_____

God Forgives

Forgive: to grant relief from payment; to pardon

Psalm 130:3-5 (NLT) LORD, if you kept a record of our sins, who, O Lord, could ever survive? But you offer forgiveness, that we might learn to fear you. I am counting on the LORD; yes, I am counting on him. I have put my hope in his word.

_____

_____

_____

God Heals

Heal: to make sound, well or healthy again; to restore; to free from grief, troubles, or evil; to reconcile; to be cured

Jeremiah 17:14 (NLT) O LORD, if you heal me, I will be truly healed; if you save me, I will be truly saved. My praises are for you alone!

_____

_____

_____

God Helps

Help: to give assistance or support; to give relief to

Psalm 121:1-2 (NLT) I look up to the mountains—does my help come from there? My help comes from the LORD, who made heaven and earth!

_____

_____

_____

God Gives Hope

Hope: to desire something with confident expectation of its fulfillment

Psalm 62:5-6 (NLT) Let all that I am wait quietly before God, for my hope is in him. He alone is my rock and my salvation, my fortress where I will not be shaken.

_____

_____

_____

God Does the Impossible

Impossible: incapable of being done, attained, fulfilled or occurring

Luke 1:37 (NLT) For nothing is impossible with God.

_____

_____

_____

God Inspires

Inspire: to breath in; to cause, guide, communicate or motivate as by divine influence

Hebrews 10:23-24 (NLT) Let us hold tightly without wavering to the hope we affirm, for God can be trusted to keep his promise. Let us think of ways to motivate one another to acts of love and good works.

_____

_____

_____

Let them praise the LORD for his great love and for the wonderful things he has done for them. Let them offer sacrifices of thanksgiving and sing joyfully about his glorious acts. Psalm 107:21-23 (NLT)

As you finish today's study, offer a sacrifice of thanksgiving to God for the many ways He demonstrates His love.

God's Character

Continue exploring the character of God. How has He demonstrated His loving care in your life or in the lives of others? Write down the ways you have seen Him work and thank Him.

God Leads

Lead: to guide by direction or example; to go first

Isaiah 48:17 (NLT) This is what the LORD says—your Redeemer, the Holy One of Israel: "I am the LORD your God, who teaches you what is good for you and leads you along the paths you should follow."

_____

_____

_____

God Lifts

Lift: to raise from a lower to a higher position; to elevate; to exert effort to overcome resistance of weight

Psalm 40:2 (NLT) He lifted me out of the pit of despair, out of the mud and the mire. He set my feet on solid ground and steadied me as I walked along.

_____

_____

_____

God Listens

Listen: to hear something with thoughtful attention

Psalm 66:17-19 (NLT) For I cried out to him for help, praising him as I spoke. If I had not confessed the sin in my heart, the Lord would not have listened. But God did listen! He paid attention to my prayer.

_____

_____

_____

God Protects

Protect: to cover or shield from exposure, injury or destruction; to guard

Proverbs 2:7-8 (NLT) He grants a treasure of common sense to the honest. He is a shield to those who walk with integrity. He guards the paths of the just and protects those who are faithful to him.

_____

_____

_____

God Redeems

Redeem: to buy back, repurchase, to rescue with a ransom

Psalm 34:22 (NLT) But the LORD will redeem those who serve him. No one who takes refuge in him will be condemned.

_____

_____

_____

God Rescues

Rescue: to free or save from danger, imprisonment or evil

Psalm 91:14-15 (NLT) The LORD says, "I will rescue those who love me. I will protect those who trust in my name. When they call on me, I will answer; I will be with them in trouble. I will rescue and honor them."

_____

_____

_____

God Restores

Restore: to renew; to revive; to bring back to a former or normal condition

1 Peter 5:10 (NLT) In his kindness God called you to share in his eternal glory by means of Christ Jesus. So after you have suffered a little while, he will restore, support, and strengthen you, and he will place you on a firm foundation.

_____

_____

_____

God Remains the Same

Same: unchanging; alike in kind, quality, amount or degree; identical

Hebrews 13:8 (NLT) Jesus Christ is the same yesterday, today, and forever.

_____

_____

_____

God Sustains

Sustain: to support or maintain; to keep in existence; to carry the weight or burden

Psalm 18:35 (NLT) You have given me your shield of victory. Your right hand supports me; your help has made me great.

_____

_____

_____

God Transforms

Transform: to change the condition, nature or character of; implies a change in either external form or in inner nature

2 Corinthians 3:17-18 (NLT) For the Lord is the Spirit, and wherever the Spirit of the Lord is, there is freedom. So all of us who have had that veil removed can see and reflect the glory of the Lord. And the Lord—who is the Spirit—makes us more and more like him as we are changed into his glorious image.

_____

_____

_____

God Understands

Understand: to comprehend; to know thoroughly; to grasp or perceive clearly and fully the nature, character or functioning; to have a sympathetic awareness

Psalm 147:5 (NLT) How great is our Lord! His power is absolute! His understanding is beyond comprehension!

_____

_____

_____

God Works

Work: to cause; to bring about; to mold, shape or form; purposeful activity

Philippians 2:13 (NLT) For God is working in you, giving you the desire and the power to do what pleases him.

_____

_____

_____

This list represents only a fraction of the ways God works in our lives. Each of these characteristics shows how God's actions are rooted in loving compassion. As you go through the day, stop and consider all the ways God is revealing His love for you. As you become aware of His acts of love, acknowledge Him and breathe a prayer of thanksgiving.

Contentment — Day Four

At one time in my working career I taught music at a private school. My goal was to do more than teach music theory, rhythms and singing. In my heart I wanted each child to learn about spiritual things through the music I taught. Each year one of my responsibilities was to present a musical program showcasing all of the children. One year I wrote a musical entitled "The Grumble Bug." It was the story of a young girl who was unhappy about almost everything. She grumbled and complained about her appearance, her family, her teachers and her friends. She was tormented within and a slave to peer pressure. Toward the end of the musical, she met a girl who had learned the meaning of contentment. The lyrics of the song she sang went like this:

True contentment comes from within.
It matters not the situation that I'm in.
When I think of how God loves me and my mind is stayed on Him
It doesn't matter what I wear,
If I have straight or curly hair,
Or who I'm with,
Or what I've done,
Or where I've been.
I am learning that true contentment only comes from within.
And now I'm free –
Free to be what Jesus wants me to be.
No longer a slave to the chains the world would place me in.
Yes, I am free –
He set me free.
And freely, I give my life to Him
For He alone brings contentment that comes from within.
It matters not the situation that I'm in.
When I think of how God loves me and my mind is stayed on Him.
I am learning that true contentment only comes from within.
True contentment comes from Him.

The Example of Paul

The account in the scriptures of the apostle Paul is an example of living a life filled with true contentment. His story reads like an adventure thriller. He makes this statement in Philippians 4:10-12 (NLT) *How I praise the Lord that you are concerned about me again. I know you have always been concerned for me, but you didn't have the chance to help me. Not that I was ever in need, for I have learned how to be content with whatever I have. I know how to live on almost nothing or with everything. I have learned the secret of living in every situation, whether it is with a full stomach or empty, with plenty or little.*

In this letter to the Philippians, Paul is thanking those who have supported him. Paul says, "I have learned the secret" of being content. When did he learn this and what is the secret? Let's take a look at Paul's journey.

Paul's Story

Paul's story is told in the book of Acts. The first mention of Paul, who at that time was named Saul, is found in Acts 7:58. Stephen, a young follower of Jesus, has infuriated the Jewish leaders with his accusations of their disobedience of God's law and resistance to the Holy Spirit. In a rage, they dragged Stephen out of the city and as they began to stone him to death, they took off his coats and laid them at the feet of Saul.

Saul was well trained in the Old Testament and sincerely believed that the Christian movement was a dangerous threat to Judasim. His intensity resulted in his personal mission to destroy the church and to kill and persecute Christians. He was traveling to Damascus, determined to arrest Christians and bring them back to Jerusalem in chains when Jesus intervened. Saul was struck blind as Jesus spoke to him from heaven giving him instructions which would lead him on a new mission. This mission would be the total opposite of Saul's passion to destroy the church. Dumbfounded, the men who accompanied Saul led him to Damascus where a believer named Ananias came to him under God's direction and prayed over him. As he prayed, Saul's eyesight was restored as God revealed the truth of the gospel. After only a few days he regained his strength and began preaching that indeed, Jesus was the Messiah, the Son of God.

From this point on, we read in the book of Acts the many situations Paul would encounter as he traveled on three missionary journeys, teaching the gospel to everyone he encountered. He did not seek a receptive audience. He preached God's message of salvation everywhere he went to those who would listen as well as those who would not hear.

Saul, who became known as Paul, encountered almost daily peril. Many times, angry mobs ran him out of town. He was stoned to the point of death, yet continued on only to be severely beaten and thrown into prison more than once. In one town after another he faced angry mobs who threatened and ridiculed him. He was brought before high city councils, governors, kings and emperors. As a prisoner in chains, he endured a terrible storm at sea, faced death at the hands of the guards, yet survived the shipwreck and then was bitten by a poisonous snake. In the last chapter of Acts, Paul is living under guard yet still preaching the gospel.

That is what Paul did. He shared what he had experienced - the power of God through faith in Jesus Christ to transform a life. Paul's transformation was so complete, all he knew was the joy of sharing the gospel. The "secret" he learned was simple. He stated it in Philippians 4:13 *For I can do everything through Christ, who gives me strength.* He experienced that "secret" every day.

Paul preached to his captors, he sang hymns and prayed while in prison and wrote letters to the churches that were filled with hope, encouragement and instruction – letters that encourage all who read them– even today.

Paul's story is a vivid example of what it means to be content even in very difficult situations. What is your situation? What is challenging your ability to be content? What is God teaching you? Do you see God at work? Write out the things that come to mind.

_____

_____

_____

_____

_____

_____

_____

_____

_____

_____

Are You Satisfied?

Contentment is being happy with what you have or who you are. If you are content you do not desire something more or different. You are satisfied. In order to acknowledge all that God has done and give Him thanks, we must be content. Yet, the enemy is always lurking around the corner trying to steal our contentment and make us a slave of the world and its counterfeit pleasures.

1 John 2:16 (NLT) *For the world offers only a craving for physical pleasure, a craving for everything we see, and pride in our achievements and possessions. These are not from the Father, but are from this world.*

Once again we see how the enemy uses one of the three points of sin. Read **Genesis 3:6** then refer to the verse above. What was the point of sin that Satan used to entice Eve to disobey God's command?

_____

Knowing that mankind could fall prey to such temptations, God included in the Ten Commandments this instruction:

Exodus 20:17 (NLT) *"You must not covet your neighbor's house. You must not covet your neighbor's wife, male or female servant, ox or donkey, or anything else that belongs to your neighbor."*

Trying to "keep up with the Joneses" or to maintain a lifestyle equal or superior to others directs our focus to material things. This is part of the enemy's playbook. When we become focused on striving to attain "things," we easily lose our focus on God's blessings. The "things" that we seek never fully satisfy and always call for more and more. True satisfaction does not come from material things or physical pleasures. It does not come from high positions or worldly esteem. True satisfaction is found within the soul and comes from knowing God. This complete satisfaction allows us to acknowledge the blessings that fill our lives. It is then that we experience contentment that leads to praise.

Psalm 63:4-5 (NLT) *I will praise you as long as I live, lifting up my hands to you in prayer. You satisfy me more than the richest feast. I will praise you with songs of joy.*

Acknowledge

Acknowledge: to state that one has received and to give thanks for

Have you ever done something nice for someone or given a gift only to have the recipient of the gift walk away without any expression of thanks? When teaching good manners to our children, one of the first things we teach is to always say "thank you." When they are so focused on the gift that they forget those important words we prompt our children to remember to express thanks. Even better than just a "thank you," however, is an acknowledgement of the generosity of the giver. That "thank you" accompanied by a hug fills the giver's heart with joy.

Acknowledge the Source

How often do we gladly receive God's blessings but fail to acknowledge the giver? Before we can truly be thankful for the blessings that fill our lives, we must acknowledge that they come from God. The source of blessings is clearly stated in James 1:17 (NIV) *Every good and perfect gift is from above, coming down from the Father of the heavenly lights, who does not change like shifting shadows.*

In this verse we see that the gifts from God are described as _____

_____

Also, God, the giver of these gifts is described as _____.

Not only should we be thankful for the gifts, we should acknowledge the character of the giver. Read **Psalm 100:1-5**

What does verse 3 call us to acknowledge about God?

_____

_____

When people came to the temple to worship God, they first came through the gates then entered the courts outside the temple. After entering through the gates, there were several courts that came closer and closer to the temple itself. Only the priests were permitted to enter the temple where they experienced the presence of God. In verse 4 we see that the worshippers entered the gates with

_____ and entered the courts with _____.

How does verse 5 describe the character of God? _____

_____

_____

Read again verses 1-2. As we acknowledge the character of God, we draw near to Him with thanksgiving and praise. It fills us with such gladness it sometimes spills out with songs and shouts of joy!

God Gives

Are you a giver or a taker? Some seem to give and give of themselves and their resources without thought of receiving anything in return. Others seem to feel entitled to be on the receiving end without thought of giving back. God is a giver. He gave life to man and gave him all of creation to inhabit and enjoy.

One line in a hymn says, "...For out of his infinite riches in Jesus, he giveth, and giveth, and giveth again." As you read the verses that follow, focus on God's giving nature. As you read them, one after another, it becomes clear that God gives to us abundantly and provides for all our needs. He gives – we receive.

Isaiah 42:5 (NLT) God, the LORD, created the heavens and stretched them out. He created the earth and everything in it. He gives breath to everyone, life to everyone who walks the earth.

Genesis 9:3 (NIV) Everything that lives and moves will be food for you. Just as I gave you the green plants, I now give you everything.

Genesis 27:20 (NIV) Isaac asked his son, "How did you find it so quickly, my son?" "The LORD your God gave me success," he replied.

Joshua 22:3 (NIV) For a long time now -- to this very day -- you have not deserted your brothers but have carried out the mission the LORD your God gave you.

Joshua 23:14 (NIV) Now I am about to go the way of all the earth. You know with all your heart and soul that not one of all the good promises the LORD your God gave you has failed. Every promise has been fulfilled; not one has failed.

2 Chronicles 15:15 (NLT) All in Judah were happy about this covenant, for they had entered into it with all their heart. They earnestly sought after God, and they found him. And the LORD gave them rest from their enemies on every side.

Psalm 94:17 (NIV) Unless the LORD had given me help, I would soon have dwelt in the silence of death.

Daniel 1:17 (NIV) To these four young men God gave knowledge and understanding of all kinds of literature and learning. And Daniel could understand visions and dreams of all kinds.

John 3:16 (NIV) For God so loved the world that he gave his one and only Son, that whoever believes in him shall not perish but have eternal life.

John 6:33 (NLT) The true bread of God is the one who comes down from heaven and gives life to the world.

John 3:34 (NLT) For he is sent by God. He speaks God's words, for God gives him the Spirit without limit.

1 Corinthians 15:57 (NLT) But thank God! He gives us victory over sin and death through our Lord Jesus Christ.

2 Thessalonians 2:16-17 (NLT) Now may our Lord Jesus Christ himself and God our Father, who loved us and by his grace gave us eternal comfort and a wonderful hope, comfort you and strengthen you in every good thing you do and say.

Romans 15:5 (NLT) May God, who gives this patience and encouragement, help you live in complete harmony with each other, as is fitting for followers of Christ Jesus.

James 1:5 (NLT) If you need wisdom, ask our generous God, and he will give it to you. He will not rebuke you for asking.

Practice Acknowledgement

The more we acknowledge God as the giver of blessings, the more of God's blessings we see. Go back and read each verse and acknowledge God's goodness with thanksgiving.

Giving Thanks in Prayer

As we complete this third step in our journey to peace, we must stop and smell the roses. We must not fall into the trap that Satan used to deceive Eve in the Garden. By causing her to focus on the one thing she could not have she lost all the blessings that surrounded her. Ask God to open your eyes to see the blessings of each day.

As we acknowledge our blessings and give thanks to God, our faith and trust in Him grows deeper. When we call out to God in prayer, then see His work in answer to prayer, it is evidence that God hears us. Often the answers are "more than we could ask or imagine."

It is difficult to imagine that we can bless God, but that is what we do when we offer thanksgiving and praise. Imagine it as a thank you with a hug. With an attitude of gratitude we praise Him and we bless Him.

Praise the LORD! For he has heard my cry for mercy. The LORD is my strength and shield. I trust him with all my heart. He helps me, and my heart is filled with joy. I burst out in songs of thanksgiving.

Psalm 28:6-7 (NLT)

Thank God for Future Victories

Thanksgiving prepares the way for God to work. We know that God is victorious. We know that He has a plan. We know that He works all things together for good. Thank Him in advance.

Week Five

Handing Over the Controls
Yield

As we continue the journey to peace, we have come to the fourth and last step. Yield. In this step we lift up our requests and concerns to God. Early in my prayer life, this was always the first step. Most of the time it was the only step I took when I prayed. Even then, it did not result in peace. Because I did not take the first step, praise, I was not focused on God. My limited knowledge of His attributes resulted in limited faith. Often I felt unworthy to voice my requests because I had neglected to take that second step of repentance. Had I taken the third step and acknowledged the evidence of God's answers to prayer, I would have been more confident as I prayed. The result was a prayer life that was shallow.

There are other words that have been used to describe this last step. Intercession is one, meaning to plead or make a request for others. Another word, supplication, is to ask for something or make a humble request as by prayer. Although these describe what is done in this step, more important than what is done is the attitude in which it is done. Unless we yield, trusting God to take control, we cannot take that last step to peace.

Control   Day One

When I am faced with a challenge or difficulty it is very hard for me to "give up." I try every way I can to offer help, to find a solution, to provide a way, to establish peace, to relieve the pain, or to understand. At times this produces at least temporary results and at other times I must admit defeat. In fact, I have come to realize that my efforts often simply delay what is best.

Often we are faced with difficulties that are totally out of our control. Although we care deeply and want relief from the stress or pain, we realize that there is nothing we can do. We do not understand. Nothing seems to make sense. We are helpless and sometimes hopeless. The Scriptures clearly show that these battles are not ours to fight. It seems that the very best thing that we can do is the very thing we find it hardest to do – "give up." Recently when I was praying about a difficult situation I am facing, I just raised my hands to the sky and said, "I give up!" The Holy Spirit spoke to my heart and I realized that I can "give" my battles "up" to the One who will always be victorious. Rather than raising up my hands in defeat, I now raise them up in victory as I yield to God. I surrender. I submit. I willingly give up control.

75

Who is in Control?

Through the years, as I have studied scripture and learned more about God's character, it has finally become clear to me that God is sovereign. His power and authority are unlimited. He is free from any external control.

Write **Psalm 115:3** _____

_____

Read **Daniel 4:35** According to this verse who can stop or question God's actions?

_____

Read **Jeremiah 32:17** What assurance does this verse give concerning God's power?

_____

As we consider these scriptures, why would we hesitate to yield control to God? Why would we presume that we have control in the first place? Read **Ephesians 6:12** What is the source of our struggle for control?

_____

_____

As we struggle with this issue of control and focus on God's character, it becomes obvious that we must yield our battles to God. He alone can defeat the enemy.

Who Fights Your Battles?

The story of David found in 1 Samuel 17 is an example of one who trusted God to fight the battle. When David, the future King of Israel, was a young boy, the Philistines and Israelites were at war. David's older brothers were soldiers in King Saul's army, but David had entered King Saul's service as an armor-bearer. He also continued to tend his father's sheep. David's father, Jesse, instructed him to take supplies to his brothers who were facing a major battle. When he arrived, David noticed that although the two armies were facing each other, no one was fighting. It was the custom at that time for one man from each army to fight so that the armies would not lose so many men. The soldier who won the fight would claim victory for his army.

The Philistines were big men and they had chosen Goliath to wage the battle. Goliath was a large, strong man. Some referred to him as a giant. No one from the Israelite army had yet come forward to fight Goliath, even after days of taunting. No one spoke a word when David asked who would be fighting the giant.

Having experienced the power of God to save him from wild animal attacks in the past, David bravely stepped forward and volunteered to fight for his people. When King Saul got word that David had volunteered, he sent for him and tried to talk him out of fighting Goliath. Having no success, he dressed David in a heavy suit of armor David could barely move, so he took it off. David had faith that God would protect him. Rather than take the big sword that was offered, David went to the stream nearby and found five smooth stones he could use with his sling shot. The Philistine army was laughing at him, but David showed no fear as he stepped forward and spoke to the giant.

1 Samuel 17:45-47 *45David replied to the Philistine, "You come to me with sword, spear, and javelin, but I come to you in the name of the LORD of Heaven's Armies—the God of the armies of Israel, whom you have defied. 46Today the LORD will conquer you, and I will kill you and cut off your head. And then I will give the dead bodies of your men to the birds and wild animals, and the whole world will know that there is a God in Israel! 47And everyone assembled here will know that the LORD rescues his people, but not with sword and spear. This is the LORD's battle, and he will give you to us!"*

David declared he did not face the giant alone. In verse 45, who did he say came with

him? _____

Write out the last sentence of verse 47.

_____

_____

David's confidence came from knowing that God would fight the battle.

Earlier in this study we read a passage from 2 Chronicles 20 where praise played an important part of defeating the enemy. Once again the account tells of a battle where the odds are against God's people. What familiar words are found at the end of 2 Chronicles 20:15?

_____

_____

What battle are you fighting? What giant are you facing? What difficulty in your life causes you pain?

_____

_____

_____

_____

_____

_____

_____

Are you trying to fight the battle alone? Have you identified the true enemy? Can you yield control to God and trust Him to fight the battle? Consider the following scriptures as you yield your burdens to God.

2 Corinthians 10:3-4 (NLT) *We are human, but we don't wage war as humans do. We use God's mighty weapons, not worldly weapons, to knock down the strongholds of human reasoning and to destroy false arguments.*

Exodus 14:14 (NLT) *The LORD himself will fight for you. Just stay calm.*

The Connection

God Hears

In this age of technology we have all sorts of gadgets that keep us connected. When I was very young our phone hung on the wall and our connection was part of a party line with four other homes. Each home had a specific "ring" that identified whose home was receiving a call. Ours was one long and four shorts. Even though the call was intended for us, anyone on the party line could pick up and listen in on the conversation. The operator in town who managed all the calls could listen in on any call she rang. She was always a good source of information for the entire community.

I remember being so excited when we moved to a new home that had a rotary dial phone. What seemed so modern then is now considered archaic. We have progressed through the years to such an extent that it is almost impossible to keep up with the newest technology. We sign up with a company, trusting their equipment and service, yet still, the connection is broken at times and calls are dropped for unknown reasons. The cell towers, cables and wireless equipment are prone to failure and important calls do not go through.

Our connection with God does not fail. If we have established a relationship with God and go to Him with a clean heart, the only time God does not hear our prayer is when we fail to pray.

Read **Isaiah 65:1** What prevents God from responding to our need for help?

_____

God Answers

In years past, phone calls were considered a priority. When the phone rang it was never ignored. Phone calls were infrequent and conversations usually were important. A big difference that I observe today when my grown children hear their cell phone ring is that they often ignore the call. They may glance at their phone to see the caller ID, but wait until it is convenient to return the call or even ignore it completely. God knows our caller ID, but He will not ignore our call. We can depend on Him to answer each time we call.

Read **Psalm 3:4** and **Psalm 34:4** What are the assurances in these verses?

_____

_____

_____

Perhaps in response to a specific prayer you have heard someone say, "God answered my prayer." Usually that means that God acted in agreement with what was prayed. There are times when we pray, when we do not see God act in agreement with our prayer. Does this mean that God has not answered our prayer? According to the scriptures, God always answers.

This reminds me of a time I was keeping my grandson. We were riding in the car and I had mentioned that after picking up his sister we *might* go to his favorite play place for lunch. Over and over again he asked, "Are we going there?" I answered, "We'll see." Again he continued to ask, "Grandma, can we have lunch there?" I answered, "We might." After several times back and forth, he finally said, "Grandma, just say YES!" It seemed that he did not think I had answered until I said "YES." That is so like us. We pray. We ask. We expect a YES. Yet there are times when we ask for things that, in God's plan, are not best. God wants what is best for us. He acts in ways that will bring about good in our lives. We don't always know what that looks like.

When we pray, we draw near to God and acknowledge that He is sovereign. We bring glory to God through prayer, for God reveals His nature and is glorified through the answers to our prayer.

When Jesus faced difficulties, when He felt concern for His disciples, when He suffered – He prayed. His example shows us that God desires that we call out to Him in prayer. In the scriptures we find that Jesus intercedes (prays) for us. The Holy Spirit intercedes when we do not know what to pray. In every case, God answers. His answer may be yes or it may be no, but He always answers. He promises to answer when we humble ourselves before Him and seek His will. Although Jesus prayed that God might spare Him from the cross, God's answer was "no" because His plan for redemption for you and for me could only be fulfilled through the death of His Son, Jesus. When we pray, we can trust that God answers – and His answer is always perfect.

What surprising statement is made in **Isaiah 65:24**?

_____

_____

Insert your name in the blanks as you read the following verse.

This is what the LORD says, he who made the earth, the LORD who formed it and established it—the LORD is his name: "Call to me, _____ , and I will answer you, _____ , and tell you great and unsearchable things you do not know."
Jeremiah 33:2-3 (NIV)

Cast your Cares   Day Three

Any concern too small to be turned into a prayer
is too small to be made into a burden.

- Corrie Ten Boom

What Should I Pray About?

The answer to this question is clear. Read **Philippians 4:6**
What does this verse say about prayer?

_____

_____

_____

Read **1 Peter 5:7** and write it out below.

_____

_____

All too often we do everything possible in order to work through our difficulties, only to we realize that we are unable to find a solution. Then, at last, we turn to God in prayer. These verses tell us that prayer is the first thing we should consider.

This High Priest of ours understands our weaknesses, for he faced all of the same testings we do, yet he did not sin. So let us come boldly to the throne of our gracious God. There we will receive his mercy, and we will find grace to help us when we need it most.

Hebrews 4:15-16 (NLT)

In this verse we see that there is nothing we can bring before God that Jesus has not experienced, so we can freely bring anything before Him and know that He wants to help us.

Cast Your Cares on Him

When I look back over the years, I see a major transformation in my prayer life. As a young child, I recited the standard prayers at bedtime and at mealtime. Although I knew that it was the right thing to do, these prayers meant very little to me. I recall becoming involved in church youth groups as I became a teenager, but my memories of those times are filled with fun activities, camps and meeting with friends on Sunday night. I have no real memory of meaningful prayer during that time. As I entered college, I found friends at the campus ministries and enjoyed the fellowship, but recall little about prayer. I know that I prayed but my prayer life was very self-centered. My prayers were more like a "laundry list" of things I felt like I needed. I do not remember offering praise to God or acknowledging His blessings. The first prayer I clearly remember was almost one year after I was married. It was then that I prayed asking Jesus to forgive me of my sin and live in my heart as Lord and Savior.

Although this prayer established a relationship with God, I still knew very little about prayer. Gradually I began to see the power of prayer as God answered prayers so specifically that it could not be explained in any other way. Although my faith was growing, prayer was still more of an exercise than an experience. I see now that though I prayed to God, I did not have the faith to trust Him because I had a very shallow knowledge of Him. I shared my concerns in prayer, then lived as though it was up to me to solve my problems. I did not know how to yield – to give up control and trust God.

In the past two decades, I have learned the power of meaningful prayer. This gradual process of learning how to pray "effectively and fervently" has transformed my life dramatically. I have come to know God in a personal way. I have experienced the freedom of knowing that God hears my confession of sin and offers forgiveness. I have become aware of God's work and His blessings in my daily life. And slowly, but surely, I have learned to yield. I have learned to "cast my cares" upon God and leave them with Him. I have learned that prayer is a constant two-way communication with God. I have seen His work and I see Him working. I have experienced true rest as I have become "yoked" with God.

Matthew 11:28-30 (NLT) *Then Jesus said, "Come to me, all of you who are weary and carry heavy burdens, and I will give you rest. Take my yoke upon you. Let me teach you, because I am humble and gentle at heart, and you will find rest for your souls. For my yoke is easy to bear, and the burden I give you is light."*

God does not promise that we will never experience burdens. In this verse, how does He promise to make our burdens bearable?

_____

Give your burdens to the LORD, and he will take care of you. He will not permit the godly to slip and fall. Psalm 55:22 (NLT)

Specific Prayer Day Four

Our prayers lay the track down on which God's power can come.
Like a mighty locomotive
His power is irresistible,
But it cannot reach us without rails.

- Watchman Nee

God Answers Specifically According to Our Need

In the Old Testament, Genesis 24 gives an account of how specific our prayers can be. Let's work through this chapter and see what it teaches us about prayer. Read **Genesis chapter 24:1-4**

What did Abraham ask his servant to do? _____

_____

In verses 5, what concern did the servant have? _____

_____

In verses 6-8, what concern did Abraham have? _____

_____

In verses 9-14, when the servant was presented with a difficult task, what did he do?

_____

How specific was his prayer? _____

_____

In verses 15-21, how quickly was his prayer answered? _____

How did the servant know that this might be the woman he was searching for?

_____

In verses 22-27, what was the last condition that must be met before the servant would know that God led him to the right woman? _____

_____

When the servant saw that God had specifically answered his prayer, what was his reaction? _____

Read verses 28-49. Here the servant tells Laban how God has answered his prayer and waits for Laban's response.

In verses 50-51, what does Laban and Bethuel's response reveal about their relationship with God? _____

What action did the servant repeat in verse 52? _____

In verses 57-58, when Rebekah's mother and brother hesitated to allow her to go, what was Rebekah's response? _____

Verses 61-67 show how God answers specific prayer. What does this passage teach you about how you should pray? _____

_____

_____

     This beautiful passage teaches us several things about prayer. It shows us that we can go to God and trust Him when faced with a difficult situation. It teaches us that specific requests can result in specific answers. All too often we fail to recognize God's work through our difficulties and when solutions come, too often we consider them to be coincidence or luck. Remember that it is God who is always at work in our lives. We also learn that God knows our needs and can answer our prayers even before we finish praying. Our part is simply to ask. The evidence of His answers may not be immediately obvious, but God is always at work. The response of the servant as he sees God's work in answer to his prayer is immediate worship. This is the appropriate response to a loving God who is always at work in our lives, leading us to victory. God's work in the hearts of Rebekah, her family members and in Isaac are examples of God's power to accomplish His plan. Specific prayer was a critical part of bringing about that plan.

Jesus Prayed Specifically

    When Jesus prayed in the garden of Gethsemane, He knew what soon would happen. He had even told the disciples that they would desert Him and deny Him. Not only that, He told them that He soon would die, be raised from the dead, and meet with them again. Although He knew that this was God's plan for the redemption of mankind, humanly, He suffered. In Matthew 26:38a as He asked His disciples to stay with Him, He told them, *"My soul is crushed with grief to the point of death."* Jesus was so sad and sorrowful, He felt like He might not survive.

    There are times when we experience deep sadness and sorrow. We are faced with difficulties and fears. It is from those experiences that specific prayers pour out from our hearts. These prayers are not like the prayers prayed at mealtime or other common occasions. These prayers expose all that is in our heart as we voice our authentic pleas for help.

The prayer Jesus prayed that night was very specific. He boldly prayed, *"My Father! If it is possible, let this cup of suffering be taken away from me."* Matthew 26:39b (NLT) It seems clear that Jesus wanted to be delivered from the difficulties He was facing.

But Jesus' prayer did not stop there. He continued, *"Yet I want your will to be done, not mine."* Matthew 26:39c (NLT)

Here we find the key to specific prayer. Following Jesus' example, we can pray specific prayers recognizing that God always wants what is best. If what we want is different from what God wants, we must trust God and yield to His perfect will. If we have established a relationship with God and know His character, we know that God's will has purpose and will result in peace.

After finding that His disciples were sleeping rather than praying for Him, Jesus went aside and prayed a second time. This time it was evident that He was becoming aligned with God's will. This time He prayed, *"My Father! If this cup cannot be taken away unless I drink it, your will be done."*

Draw Close to God

How do we come to the point where we trust God enough to pray specifically, then yield to God's will? When a similar question was asked recently in a Bible study I attended, I simply replied, "You become old." Seriously, some of my dear friends agree. It takes time – time studying God's word, experiencing His faithfulness, and learning to know and trust Him throughout life. For some this knowledge comes quickly. For others, it comes gradually until you finally realize the truth of God's love and the perfection of His will. Finally you know that He always wants what is best. What is best is known by God alone.

Read **John 15:7**. What conditions are stated as a prerequisite for receiving anything you ask?

_____

_____

Pray About Everything

What are your specific prayer requests? Boldly bring the problem to God and leave it in His hands. Yield. Trust God as He works according to His purpose.

_____

_____

_____

_____

_____

_____

Praying Scripture

God's Armor

Earlier in this study we identified the "armor of God" as found in Ephesians 6:10-17. The enemy attempts to defeat us in many different ways, but one of the most effective is when Satan accuses us. The Breastplate of Righteousness is our defense when the enemy uses guilt as his weapon of defeat. It is by God's righteousness that we hold the key to victory.

Read **Hebrews 10:19-23** Because of the blood of Jesus, how can we approach God

in prayer? _____

What does verse 22 say about our guilt? _____

_____

Although we have established that when we confess, God will forgive our sin, Satan does not give up but focuses his attacks in the battlefield of the mind. We must make sure that we are protected with the full armor. We must be equipped with the belt of truth so that we can refuse the lies that the enemy will feed us. We must accompany the gospel of peace with the shield of faith. When we maintain a peaceful spirit, trusting in God, we will not fall to fear or doubt.

As you read the following passage from Ephesians 6:11-14 (NLT) underline what we are instructed to do as we put on God's protective armor.

Put on all of God's armor so that you will be able to stand firm against all strategies of the devil. For we are not fighting against flesh-and-blood enemies, but against evil rulers and authorities of the unseen world, against mighty powers in this dark world, and against evil spirits in the heavenly places. Therefore, put on every piece of God's armor so you will be able to resist the enemy in the time of evil. Then after the battle you will still be standing firm. Stand your ground, putting on the belt of truth and the body armor of God's righteousness.

All of the pieces of armor that have been mentioned are defensive. They are designed to protect from attack. According to this passage, we are prepared for the battle, but rather than fight we are simply to stand firm. This was the instruction that was given to the Israelites when they were pursued by the Egyptian army in Exodus 14:13-15 (NLT). *But Moses told the people, "Don't be afraid. Just stand still and watch the LORD rescue you today. The Egyptians you see today will never be seen again. The LORD himself will fight for you. Just stay calm."*

The last part of the armor mentioned in Ephesians 6 is the sword of the Spirit, which is the Word of God. This is the only piece of the armor that is used for attack. The Word of God is the offensive weapon used to defeat the enemy. Now we will see how we can use this effective weapon as we pray.

Scripture

2 Timothy 3:16 (NLT) *All Scripture is inspired by God and is useful to teach us what is true and to make us realize what is wrong in our lives. It corrects us when we are wrong and teaches us to do what is right.*

We are blessed that God has revealed His inspired Word to us in the Bible. The Bible is a treasure filled with truths that will enable us to know God and live a life filled with joy and peace. According to **2 Timothy 3:16**, what are the practical uses of the scriptures?

1) _____

2) _____

3) _____

4) _____

When God Speaks to Us

Prayer is a two way communication, not a monologue. "How," you may ask, "does God speak to me?" The Scriptures reveal that God listens to us when we call out to Him. He hears our cries and responds. But do we hear God when He speaks? Many times our days are so filled with the "noises" of everyday life that we do not hear God's voice. What would a day be like if, even for just a few moments, we turned off the radios, the phones and televisions and expectantly listened for God's voice?

Read **Psalm 50:1** Who does God speak to and when does He speak?

_____

_____

God speaks to us in many different ways. Read **Job 33:14-15** How often does God speak and in what ways? Why do we not hear Him?

_____

_____

Even as we go about our work, if we listen, might we hear God's voice? According to the following verse, does God speak to us?

_____

Psalm 85:8a (NLT) *"I listen carefully to what God the LORD is saying, for he speaks peace to his faithful people."*

God speaks to those who know Him and are faithful to Him. We recognize His voice by becoming familiar with His Word and His character. Just as we recognize the voice of someone we know, we will recognize God's voice if we listen.

God speaks peace. Peace of heart. Peace of mind. He gives counsel, direction and speaks comfort. He corrects and encourages. God speaks. Listen for His voice.

When We Speak to God

God speaks to us through His Word. We speak to God in prayer. It our connecting link. Yet there are times when we simply don't know what to say. There are situations we face that are beyond our understanding. There are times of weakness that overwhelm us. There are moments of joy that leave us speechless. What are we to do – what can we say – how can we communicate with God? In these times when we are at a loss, there is one perfect place that we will find the key to communicating what we hold in our hearts as we continue our journey to peace.

Just as a young child learns to speak and communicate by hearing new words, then speaking them back to those who are teaching him, we learn effective communication with God by speaking His Word back to Him. As we try to communicate what is in our heart, praying scripture enables us to communicate with God on a much deeper level. As we pray, we are not just telling God what He already knows or reciting a list of wants or needs, we are speaking His Word, repeating His promises, and claiming His victory. When we pray God's Word we can be assured that we are praying according to His will. Praying Scripture communicates with God in a way that brings hope.

Examples of Scriptural Prayer

God's Word is personal. It is His message, written and preserved through thousands of years, just for you. When you read each verse, God is speaking to you. Because it is personal, it can be applied to everyday situations that you experience. As you pray His word, yield the situation to Him.

The Scriptures that follow are examples of how Scriptures can be prayed back to God. Blanks have been added for you to insert your name or the name of the one for whom you are praying. Some verses are examples of yielding your need to God. Others are examples of God's Word that are prayed in faith that God will work out His word in the life of the individual. These examples represent only a few of the wealth of Scriptures that can be prayed. With an attitude of prayer and faith, speak these verses to God. Let His Word pour over you and those you are praying for and put your trust in the truth of God's Word.

God Encourages

May our Lord Jesus Christ himself and God our Father, who loved _____ and by his grace gave _____ eternal encouragement and good hope, encourage _____'s heart and strengthen _____ in every good deed and word. 2 Thessalonians 2:16-17 (NIV)

God is Faithful

But the Lord is faithful, and he will strengthen and protect you, _____, from the evil one. May the Lord direct your heart, _____, into God's love and Christ's perseverance. 2 Thessalonians 3:3,5 (NIV)

God Finishes

And I am certain, _____, that God, who began the good work within you, _____, will continue his work until it is finally finished on the day when Christ Jesus returns. Philippians 1:6 (NLT)

God Forgives

...open _____'s eyes and turn _____ from darkness to light, and from the power of Satan to God, so that _____ may receive forgiveness of sins and a place among those who are sanctified by faith ... Acts 26:18-19 (NIV)

God Guides

Show _____ your ways, O Lord, teach _____ your paths; guide _____ in your truth and teach _____, for you are God _____'s Savior, and _____'s hope is in you all day long. Psalm 25:4-5(NIV)

God Keeps

Oh, that you would bless _____ indeed, and enlarge _____'s territory, that your hand would be with _____ , and that you would keep _____ from evil, that _____ may not cause pain. 1 Chronicles 4:10 ((NIV The prayer of Jabez)

God is our Peace

Peace I leave with you, _____; my peace I give you. I do not give to you as the world gives. Do not let your heart be troubled, _____, and do not be afraid. John 14:27(NIV)

God Protects

Do not withhold your mercy from _____, O LORD; may your love and your truth always protect _____. Psalm 40:11(NIV)

God Redeems

Keep your servant, _____, also from willful sins; may they not rule over _____. Then will _____ be blameless, innocent of great transgression. May the words of _____'s mouth and the meditation of _____'s heart be pleasing in your sight, O LORD, _____'s rock and _____'s redeemer. Psalm 19:13-14(NIV)

God Restores

Do not cast _____ from your presence or take your Holy Spirit from _____.
Restore to _____ the joy of your salvation and grant _____ a willing spirit, to
sustain _____. Psalm 51:11-12(NIV)

God Speaks

But I will reveal my name to _____, and _____ will come to know its power. Then
at last _____ will recognize that I am the one who speaks to them. Isaiah 52:6 (NLT)

God is Victorious

For the LORD your God is going with you, _____! He will fight for you, _____,
against your enemies, and he will give you, _____, victory! Deuteronomy 20:4(NLT)

This last step leading to peace can be the most difficult. As we take this step we are entering into unknown territory. The only assurance of our destination lies in trusting God to bring us to a place of peace. The trip may be quick or it may take much longer than we expect. As we go, we must give up control. In doing so we must put away our pre-conceived ideas of what the final outcome may be. We must have a strong connection with God and ask for His help, yielding to His will. We cannot hold back. We must cast all of our cares on God – specific and detailed. When we are at a loss for words, we can pray God's Word – the source of supply for every need.

As we do all of this, we must "give up." We must "give" our cares "up" to Him. As we yield to God, He leads us to peace.

Week Six

Final Destination
Peace

Have you ever taken a trip and found that the final destination was different than you imagined it would be? The peace that God gives is unlike any other. In this last week of our study, let's explore all the facets of the final destination.

Trust

Now that we have completed the four steps that lead to peace, there may be a few bumps in the road that we must consider. Although we come before Him with praise and repentance, acknowledging His mighty works and yielding our cares to Him, there are times when we must wait and trust God as He accomplishes His perfect plan. Unless we put our trust in Him, the journey to peace will be delayed.

Are We There Yet?

I remember traveling with my daughter and grandchildren through west Texas one spring to a destination over seven hours away. There was not much to see along the road except hundreds of windmills dotted throughout the fields. Several times my three year old grandson asked, "When will we get there?" The concept of a trip taking several hours was unfamiliar to this little one who was used to living in the city. After a nap, he awoke and looked out at the same scenery he had seen earlier and calmly said, "Looks like this is gonna take a while."

The impatient child who wants to quickly reach the final destination of a journey often repeatedly asks, "Are we there yet?" Over and over they ask, never satisfied with any answer other than, "Yes, we are here!" There are times when our journey to peace seems longer than it should. What we don't realize is that even though we do not see the answer to our prayer, we can still arrive at our destination if we simply trust that God is at work.

All too often we are in a hurry. We hastily move about, sometimes carelessly and recklessly. We want things done rapidly. We want solutions and answers that will make us feel comfortable.

God does not hurry.

He teaches us to wait.

It is not that God takes pleasure in torturing us by holding back His answers to our prayers. It is simply that His answers are perfectly timed according to His perfect purpose. To wait while trusting God is to remain in readiness or in anticipation until we see His finished work.

Are you in God's waiting room? Are there prayers you have prayed for days, months, even years that you have not seen answered? The scriptures are clear, that when we wait on God, He will be faithful to act and He wants good things for us. Our timetable may not be the same as His, but we can trust that He will not act in haste. His answers are perfectly timed. It is in the waiting room that our faith can grow as we wait in expectation for His answer. It is there that we can say to Him, "I trust you." As you pray and wait for God, find hope in Him, knowing that He will not act hastily or too quickly, but with perfect timing to bless you with what is best.

Read **Psalm 27:13-14**. What do these verses tell us that we will see if we wait

patiently for God? _____

Waiting = Trusting

The story of Abraham is found in Genesis 12:1-25:18. At the age of 75, God spoke to Abraham and promised to make his descendants into a great nation. It was not until he was 99 years old that God confirmed that Sarah, Abraham's 90 year old wife, would give birth to a son. Even though he made many mistakes throughout those years, Abraham trusted God, waiting for His promise to be fulfilled.

In Paul's letter to the Romans, he referred to Abraham as one who waited and trusted God.

Romans 4:18-21(NLT) *Even when there was no reason for hope, Abraham kept hoping— believing that he would become the father of many nations. For God had said to him, "That's how many descendants you will have!" And Abraham's faith did not weaken, even though, at about 100 years of age, he figured his body was as good as dead—and so was Sarah's womb. Abraham never wavered in believing God's promise. In fact, his faith grew stronger, and in this he brought glory to God. He was fully convinced that God is able to do whatever he promises.*

Later, God tested Abraham, asking him to do the unthinkable. God asked Abraham to sacrifice his son Isaac as a burnt offering. This was the son God had promised. The one who would continue Abraham's lineage. Still believing and trusting in God's promise, Abraham prepared to sacrifice Isaac.

Read **Genesis 22:9-18**

What encouragement does verse 14 give us? _____

In verses 15-18 God promises His _____

because of Abraham's _____.

90

When Doubts Arise

Have you ever suffered from a bad case of the "what ifs?"   One of the enemy's tactics is to squeeze into our thoughts just a sliver of doubt. Read **Genesis 3:1-6**

How did Satan twist the truth in verse 1?_____

_____

In verse 2-3, Eve correctly states the command given by God. Then in verses 4-5, Satan effectively plants doubts in Eve's mind. What does he imply?

_____

_____

Now Eve is faced with the question, "What if this is true?" She has a choice to make. Satan has effectively planted a seed of doubt and we see Eve falling prey to the three points of sin. Write the phrases in verse 6 that illustrate each point.

Physical desires _____

Material desires _____

Pride _____

When we find ourselves in the "waiting room," there are times when we begin to have doubts. It seems as though God is silent. These doubts can lead to the "what ifs" causing our trust in God to falter. Satan will be waiting on our doorstep, ready to walk right in and fuel those doubts if we are not prepared. When doubts arise we must ask ourselves, "What is true?"

All too often, rather than focusing on the truth of God, we become focused on our circumstances. This allows Satan an opportunity to take advantage of our doubts and fill us with fear. This is the time that we must use our offensive weapon against the lies of the enemy. We must go to God's Word and be reminded of the truth. It is the only sure cure for the "what ifs."

Read the following scriptures and write the truth found in God's Word.

2 Samuel 7:28 _____

Psalm 9:9-10 _____

Psalm 62:5-6 _____

Luke 1:37 _____

Romans 8:28 _____

When the enemy tries to "shake you up" with doubts and fill you with "what ifs" claim the truth of God found in Psalm 16:8 (NIV) *I keep my eyes always on the LORD. With him at my right hand, I will not be shaken.*

I Believe

I have a vivid memory of a day when my faith was tested. I was a young mother, sitting by my best friend in a church service. The pastor asked for those who were willing to commit their life totally to God to stand up. Immediately my friend shot up out of her seat. Although I loved God, I was hesitant. I sat there, unable to stand, considering all that such an action would imply. I have since grown in my faith and now realize that I can trust God in all things – today and in the future.

If you were to rate your trust in God on the following scale, considering your willingness to commit your life totally to God, where would it fall?

0	1	2	3	4	5	6	7	8	9	10

Unwilling	Somewhat	Totally Willing

God has a plan and a purpose in all things. If we believe the truth of God's Word, that He loves us and wants good things for us as His Word says, why would we hesitate to trust Him? Is it because we do not believe? Is it possible to "somewhat" believe? Is it because Satan has planted doubts that have taken root?

When we focus on who God is and learn about His character, when we see Him working in our lives, when we understand His perfect unfailing love it becomes clear that we can trust Him in all things. Our heart's cry becomes, "I believe!"

Trust and Obey

The words "trust" and "obey" are found in an old hymn. The line in the chorus goes, "Trust and obey, for there's no other way to be happy in Jesus, but to trust and obey." In order to obey, we must first trust. When Eve was deceived and did not trust what God commanded, it resulted in that first step of disobedience. That first step led mankind down the path of sin and death, rather than the path of fellowship and peace that God intended. Throughout the scriptures we see the consequences suffered by those who did not obey the commands of God as well as the blessings experienced by those who trusted Him. We show God how much we love Him when we trust and obey Him. He is worthy of our trust.

Having this assurance that God is trustworthy gives us peace as we enter our final destination.

We wait in hope for the LORD; he is our help and our shield. In him our hearts rejoice, for we trust in his holy name. Psalm 33:20-21 (NLT)

Hope is a force that keeps us moving forward. Without hope, purpose fades and the future grows dim. In God's Word we find encouragement, help, wisdom, truth and so much more that fills us with hope. Even when we face situations that we cannot understand, and are unable to imagine how they will be resolved, we can be hopeful knowing that God has a plan and that He is working in all things to benefit those who love Him. Keeping focused on God's truth and trusting Him, we can press on with confidence and with hope.

God's Word is a Source of Hope

Romans 15:4 (NLT) *Such things were written in the Scriptures long ago to teach us. And the Scriptures give us hope and encouragement as we wait patiently for God's promises to be fulfilled.*

The wealth of encouragement found in the Scriptures is available at any time that we might feel hopeless. Perhaps one of the most encouraging verses is found in Jeremiah 29:11 (NLT). In this verse we are encouraged as we read, *"For I know the plans I have for you," says the LORD. "They are plans for good and not for disaster, to give you a future and a hope."* The promise of a good, hopeful future fills our hearts with peace. The only thing that can steal that peace is fear. Because the enemy knows that fear is a powerful weapon, Satan uses it often and effectively.

I asked several of my friends to answer in one word the question, "What it is that holds you back from reaching out or trying a new venture or stepping into unknown territory?" The answer was always the same. "Fear." Wanting to explore this further, I went to the Scriptures and found something very thought provoking.

Fear Not

Let's look at the meaning of the word, "fear." Just as so many other words in the English language, "fear" has more than one definition. First it is defined as "a feeling of alarm, terror, dread or apprehension." Surely this is not what is meant when we are commanded to fear God. The second definition of fear, however, complies with the command to fear God. This definition is "extreme reverence or awe." Hebrews 12:28 (NLT) illustrates this clearly: *Since we are receiving a Kingdom that is unshakable, let us be thankful and please God by worshiping him with holy fear and awe.* This "fear" leads us to hope and peace.

All too often the fear described first is what we experience - the fear that paralyzes us. This is revealed in Psalm 143:3-5 (NLT) *My enemy has chased me. He has knocked me to the ground and forces me to live in darkness like those in the grave. I am losing all hope; I am paralyzed with fear.* How can we overcome this paralyzing fear? We find the answer in the Scriptures.

Read **Genesis 3:6-10**

Before this time, Adam and Eve felt no shame. They enjoyed a relationship with God and were blessed. The fear they experienced was one of "reverence and awe." Things changed dramatically when they disobeyed God. In verse 10, what emotional response did Adam give when God called for him in the garden?

_____

The fear that paralyzes with alarm and apprehension became a reality. When sin entered the world, fear was its companion. It has remained so until this day. The root of this dreaded emotion seems to be the issue of control. When we are not in control, we experience apprehension, dread, even terror. As the verses in Psalm 143 stated, we are "forced to live in darkness."

So, did God just leave us in this sad state of affairs? Absolutely not! God – our awesome, loving God, full of grace, put into motion His provision to restore the original type of fear that man experienced before sin entered the world – the fear that bursts forth as reverence and awe. But He asked us once again to be obedient. In order to overcome the fear expressed as dread and experience the fear which is expressed as reverence and awe, we must give up control. Indeed, we must "face our fear." The very thing that causes fear, giving up control, is what God requires. We must trust God.

Now, fast forward to a scene that reveals God's love and compassion. I imagine it as a still, cool, clear night in the hills around Bethlehem. The shepherds are tending their sheep. All is peaceful and quiet until suddenly in the sky there is a commotion unlike any other in all of history. The sky is illuminated and an angel of the Lord appears. The shepherds are terrified! They are apprehensive! They are filled with dread! They are filled with fear! And what are the first words they hear from the voice of the angel?

Read **Luke 2:8-10** _____

God filled the heavens with the proclamation that He would deliver us from our apprehension, our dread, and our terror. He set into motion the provision that would forever free us from those fears. His plan was revealed as the angel announced the birth of the Savior, Jesus Christ. With this announcement, a host of angels praised God declaring in Luke 2:14, _"Glory to God in the highest heaven and _____ on earth to those with whom God is pleased."_ God asks us to trust Him, to be obedient to Him and to give up control by accepting His provision, Jesus Christ. He is the one who comes to deliver us from our sin and our fears and give us peace. The result is to experience the fear of God that Adam enjoyed at the beginning of creation. With reverence and awe as we worship a loving God, we are filled with peace and hope is restored.

God's Love is Unfailing

Take delight in the LORD, and he will give you your heart's desires. Commit everything you do to the LORD. Trust him, and he will help you. Psalm 37:4-5 (NLT)

The four steps we have taken give us the freedom to hope. When we are hopeful, we are free to express a desire with confident expectation of its fulfillment. This confidence can be sure only if it is rooted in our faith and trust in God.

Psalm 33:21-22 (NLT) *In him our hearts rejoice, for we trust in his holy name. Let your unfailing love surround us, LORD, for our hope is in you alone.*

What does this scripture suggest is the reason for our confidence?

_____

Read **Psalm 147:11** What gives delight to the Lord?_____

_____

We wait in hope for the Lord; he is our help and our shield. In him our hearts rejoice, for we trust in is holy name. May your unfailing love rest upon us, O Lord, even as we put our hope in you. Psalm 33:20-22 (NIV)

Rest

The prayer of the feeblest saint on earth
who lives in the spirit and keeps right with God
is a terror to Satan.
The very powers of darkness are paralyzed by prayer...
No wonder Satan tries to keep our minds fussy in active work
till we cannot think in prayer.

- Oswald Chambers

Rest is Required

Rest is one of the great benefits we enjoy as our final destination, peace, surrounds us. It is an important part of our journey that the enemy would want to keep us from experiencing.

In His perfect design, God created the human body with a need for rest. Without it, the body will cease to function. The importance of rest is shown in the Scriptures.

Read Genesis 2:2

What example did God give us at the completion of creation?

_____

Read **Psalm 121:3-4** What does this tell you about God's need for rest?

_____

Although God does not need rest, He gave us the example of rest knowing that without it the responsibilities of work and family would keep our body exhausted, our mind churning and our spirit in turmoil. He found it so important, that it was one of the Ten Commandments given to Moses.

Read Exodus 20:8-11

According to this commandment, in what way are we to consider this day of rest?

_____

_____

Read **Mark 2:27** Write the words that Jesus spoke.

_____

_____

Here again, we see that God designed our bodies with a need for rest and that it is for our benefit that we observe this day to rest. We honor God by obeying Him. When our bodies and minds are at rest, we are better able to focus on Him and find the spiritual peace that comes from God alone.

Unlimited Rest

The rest that God offers is not limited to one day. We can enjoy God's rest moment by moment if we maintain our focus on God. Even in the midst of troubles, the rest that God offers can fill our body, mind and spirit.

The beautiful passage found in Psalm 91 is very special to me. This is the passage that my father read over and over as he experienced combat in World War II. When I hear the stories of how he landed on the beach on D-Day 3, drove over icy fields filled with mines, and slowly crossed Europe for two years facing the enemy, I am amazed at God's protection that preserved his life. In the midst of constant peril, God's Word is where my father found rest.

As you read this Psalm, focus on the rest that God gives to all who choose to receive.

Psalm 91 (NLT)

Those who live in the shelter of the Most High will find rest in the shadow of the Almighty. This I declare about the LORD: He alone is my refuge, my place of safety; he is my God, and I trust him. For he will rescue you from every trap and protect you from deadly disease. He will cover you with his feathers. He will shelter you with his wings. His faithful promises are your armor and protection. Do not be afraid of the terrors of the night, nor the arrow that flies in the day. Do not dread the disease that stalks in darkness, nor the disaster that strikes at midday. Though a thousand fall at your side, though ten thousand are dying around you, these evils will not touch you. Just open your eyes, and see how the wicked are punished.

If you make the LORD your refuge, if you make the Most High your shelter, no evil will conquer you; no plague will come near your home. For he will order his angels to protect you wherever you go. They will hold you up with their hands so you won't even hurt your foot on a stone. You will trample upon lions and cobras; you will crush fierce lions and serpents under your feet!

The LORD says, "I will rescue those who love me. I will protect those who trust in my name. When they call on me, I will answer; I will be with them in trouble. I will rescue and honor them. I will reward them with a long life and give them my salvation."

Rest is God's Gift

Job 3:25-26 (NLT) *What I always feared has happened to me. What I dreaded has come true. I have no peace, no quietness. I have no rest; only trouble comes.*

God does not promise a life free of pain. He does promise that even in the midst of the pain we can experience His rest. I was listening to a newscast one evening and a family who was going through very difficult circumstances was being interviewed. The reporter was emphasizing the tragedy of the story. When the reporter asked how he was feeling, the man replied, "Pain is unavoidable. Misery is optional."

It is when we focus on our difficult circumstances that we deny the gift of rest that God offers. We have a choice. We can choose to be miserable or, even in the midst of pain we can accept this invitation:

Matthew 11:28-30 (NLT) *Then Jesus said, "Come to me, all of you who are weary and carry heavy burdens, and I will give you rest. Take my yoke upon you. Let me teach you, because I am humble and gentle at heart, and you will find rest for your souls. For my yoke is easy to bear, and the burden I give you is light."*

When we choose to become yoked with God, the result is rest. This rest includes peace of mind, spirit and body.

Psalm 16:7-9 (NLT) *I will praise the LORD, who counsels me; even at night my heart instructs me. I have set the LORD always before me. Because he is at my right hand, I will not be shaken. Therefore my heart is glad and my tongue rejoices; my body also will rest secure.*

Listen

Rest gives us time to listen. When my grandson was about four years old he said to his mother, "I hear God speak to me."

Somewhat surprised, she asked, "You do? What does He say?"

Very calmly he replied, "He tells me He loves me."

Oh, that we could become as a child and in the midst of the chaos of life to stop – rest – listen – and hear God's voice. He is telling us, "I love you." In this we find true rest.

This final destination – peace – is becoming a reality.

Victory

God is Victorious

There is one last thought we must consider before we complete our journey to peace. This fact must become a declaration that we choose to make, moment by moment as we continue our journey.

"God IS victorious."

So often when we face the battles in our lives we are so focused on the conflict, we fail to acknowledge the sure victory that is set before us. This prevents us from arriving at our destination. When Jesus died on the cross He declared, "It is finished!" The battle of the ages had been fought. Sin and death were defeated.

When I have faced the battles of life, there have been times when I thought, "Who am I to stand against Satan?" During these times I have experienced defeat. Unable to see any way I could overcome the lies and attacks that Satan had forced upon me, I was miserable. My misery was due to the fact that I had no vision of victory. My only vision was that of defeat. Then a new thought filled my mind. "Who is Satan to stand against God?" The enemy IS defeated. I must surrender, but not to defeat. I must surrender to God and trust Him. When I choose to claim the victory that He has won, I am filled with hope. As I look to the future, I am filled with peace.

We must not trust in our efforts to claim victory, we must acknowledge the FACT that God is victorious – always. Yes, the enemy is defeated. Satan *cannot* and *will not* win. The battle is not ours, it is God's. When we allow God to go before us and stand in Him, victory is certain. God is victorious!

The Road to Victory

As we travel the road to victory in our journey to peace, even with the certainty of victory, we must realize that we will face battles. Victory does not come without a battle. This is true in sports, in war and especially in the spiritual realm. Although the enemy is defeated, Satan does all that is possible to cause us to join him in defeat. If the enemy can cause our vision to become so clouded with the force of battle that we lose sight of our victory, he has succeeded in bringing us down. When we choose to change the way we think about these battles, the enemy has no power.

Often as I consider how God works in our lives, I try to push aside my usual thought processes and attempt to find new ways to think. As I was considering the concept of the trials that we face as well as the blessings we experience, I discovered a new way of thinking.

A New Way of Thinking

Read **James 1:2-3**

In verse 2, James tells us that we should face trials in what manner?

_____

In verse 3, he states that these trials are a _____ of our faith that

increases our perseverance.

In a letter to the Romans, Paul expresses this same view.

Romans 5:3-5 (NLT) *We can rejoice, too, when we run into problems and trials, for we know that they help us develop endurance. And endurance develops strength of character, and character strengthens our confident hope of salvation. And this hope will not lead to disappointment. For we know how dearly God loves us, because he has given us the Holy Spirit to fill our hearts with his love.*

Generally when things are going smoothly in our lives, we consider these to be times of blessing. When we face difficulties, often we consider these times as trials. Now let's try to think of it in a different way. What if the difficulties that we face are the times of blessing and the times when things are going smoothly are the times of trials?

Before you shake your head, let me explain. When life is easy and everything is going smoothly, often our tendency is to become complacent. We become confident and self sufficient, at times focusing more on what we call the "blessings" of life. Our dependence upon God may waver and our relationship with Him may become stagnant.

On the other hand, when we are faced with the "trials" of life, one of the first things we do is turn to God for help. Consider the actions of those who find themselves in dangerous circumstances. Often, when faced with disaster or possible death, people call out to God for help without hesitation, knowing that He alone is able to save them.

Many times the questions are asked, "Why does God allow the "trials" of life?" "How could a loving God allow these things to happen?" Now this is my question – when is it that we call out to God and most strongly experience His presence? Is it during the times of "blessing" or the times of "trial?" Could it be that God wants us to experience the fullness of His presence so clearly that He allows these "trials" which in reality pour out the "blessings" of His presence?

But then, you may ask, "How do the "blessings" become the "trials." The first definition of "trial" is "the act of testing." Perhaps the times of blessing are a time of testing our faith. Do we maintain an intimate relationship with God during the good times? Do we experience the fullness of His presence through worship and prayer? Do we read His Word and grow in our faith and knowledge of Him? During these good times, do we draw closer to God?

When difficult times come, try a new way of thinking. God wants to bless you with an awareness of His presence and power. He is there to help you. He loves you. The "blessings" of God's presence that you experience during the difficult times will bring about hope and peace. Then, when God has proven Himself to be sufficient to meet your need, get ready for the trial that will follow. Will you continue to focus on your relationship with God in the good times as well? True peace, joy and fulfillment can be found in Him alone. With this new way of thinking, when the difficult times come your way, consider it a reminder to focus on God, the One who is faithful, the One who is sufficient, the One who is in control, and more than anything, the One who longs to have fellowship with you. Then bless God by maintaining that intimate relationship. What once was considered a "trial" will lose its power as the focus on God brings a constant awareness of His presence.

The ultimate desire of God is that we know Him - truly know Him and have a personal relationship with Him – just as He planned in the beginning. God loves us so much that He will do whatever is necessary to take us to that place. No one looks forward to difficult times, yet often it is then when we experience the greatest awareness of God's sufficiency. It is often during these times that God's provision of grace is a strong witness to others who need Him. It is then that we experience true victory.

Read **Deuteronomy 20:4**, **Psalm 60:12**, and **Proverbs 21:30-31**

What clear message is found in each of these verses?

_____

_____

Underline that same message found in the following verse.

Psalm 44:6-8(NLT) *I do not trust in my bow; I do not count on my sword to save me. You are the one who gives us victory over our enemies; you disgrace those who hate us. O God, we give glory to you all day long and constantly praise your name.*

Our Victory Brings Glory to God

Psalm 20:1, 4-5a (NLT) *In times of trouble, may the LORD answer your cry. May the name of the God of Jacob keep you safe from all harm. May he grant your heart's desires and make all your plans succeed. May we shout for joy when we hear of your victory and raise a victory banner in the name of our God.*

It thrills me when I hear those who are victorious proclaim "Glory to God." It is when we recognize that God is the One who fights the battle and that His victory is sure that we declare His glory. When we do, we are inspiring all those who hear us that God will lead to victory all who trust in Him.

Psalm 145:4-6 (NLT) *Let each generation tell its children of your mighty acts; let them proclaim your power. I will meditate on your majestic, glorious splendor and your wonderful miracles. Your awe-inspiring deeds will be on every tongue; I will proclaim your greatness.*

When victory is declared it is followed by peace.

Day Five   Peace

Final Destination

As we settle down in this place of peace, we enjoy a growing, intimate relationship with God. This place fills our hearts with a knowledge of God's character that spills out in praise. We are cleansed and forgiven of our sin. We are keenly aware of God's work in our lives and acknowledge His bountiful blessings. The cares that burden our hearts, we willingly yield to God. Our hearts are filled with trust and with hope; we are at rest and we are victorious. We are at peace – a state of calm, quiet and tranquility; free from strife or discord.

When you started this study, perhaps you had a vision of what the final destination would look like. You may have been searching for answers to questions or problems you are experiencing. You may have looked for healing of body or spirit. Perhaps you sought relief from burdens that overwhelm you. Although solutions to any of these circumstances can bring a measure of peace, there is only one peace that is lasting and does not depend on our circumstances. That peace comes from knowing and trusting God.

The following verses describe the benefits that accompany God's perfect peace. Underline the phrases that illustrate these benefits.

Psalm 29:11 The LORD gives strength to his people; the LORD blesses his people with peace.

Psalm 119:165 Great peace have they who love your law, and nothing can make them stumble.

Proverbs 16:7 When a man's ways are pleasing to the LORD, he makes even his enemies live at peace with him.

Isaiah 32:17 The fruit of righteousness will be peace; the effect of righteousness will be quietness and confidence forever.

Isaiah 54:10 Though the mountains be shaken and the hills be removed, yet my unfailing love for you will not be shaken nor my covenant of peace be removed, says the Lord, who has compassion on you.

John 14:27 Peace I leave with you; my peace I give you. I do not give to you as the world gives. Do not let your heart be troubled and do not be afraid.

John 16:33 I have told you these things, so that in me you may have peace. In this world you will have trouble. But take heart! I have overcome the world.

God is Personal

Psalm 139:1-6 (NLT) *O LORD, you have examined my heart and know everything about me. You know when I sit down or stand up. You know my thoughts even when I'm far away. You see me when I travel and when I rest at home. You know everything I do. You know what I am going to say even before I say it, LORD. You go before me and follow me. You place your hand of blessing on my head. Such knowledge is too wonderful for me, too great for me to understand!*

In the past few years I have grown keenly aware that when I focus on God and His fullness, I am filled with peace – regardless of the circumstances that surround me. It was not until recently that I realized that *He is focused on me*. That thought overwhelms me. The scriptures reveal the personal nature of God. He designed me in the womb. He knows me intimately right down to the number of hairs on my head. He knows where I am and the path I will take. He is listening to my every prayer. He knows my heart and my thoughts. He knows and provides for my every need, whether it is physical or spiritual. He is personally focused on me – and focused on you. Knowing these things is a great source of peace.

Maintaining Peace

As Jesus explained in John 14:27, the peace we experience from God is unlike any other, for it is constant, even when turmoil surrounds us. Read **Philippians 4:7** How is this peace described?

The peace that we experience is a product of our relationship with God. As we maintain our relationship with God, the peace we experience will be maintained as well. By nurturing our relationship with God the peace we experience will grow to such an extent that, just as the scripture describes, it will be beyond our understanding.

How do we nurture our relationship with God and experience this growing peace? We communicate with Him. Colossians 4:2 tells us, *"Devote yourselves to prayer with an alert mind and a thankful heart."*

God speaks to us through His Word, and we speak to Him through prayer. When this communication becomes a constant part of our everyday life we enjoy the benefits of our relationship. The treasures of the Scripture add new dimensions to our faith, and through prayer we can always be in close communication with God. When God becomes our focus, we are filled with peace.

Read **Isaiah 26:3** What two factors lead us to "perfect peace?"

1) _____   2) _____

Have you ever found yourself reading the Bible only to finish and have no idea what you just read? Or perhaps when praying, your mind wanders to the tasks of the day or other thoughts. It is important that we have a clear focus and an alert mind as we communicate with God. The enemy will take every opportunity to slip in and try to scramble our messages and take away our peace.

Romans 12:12 *Be joyful in hope, patient in affliction, faithful in prayer.*

God's Word – Our Treasure

Job 23:10-12 (NLT) *"But he knows where I am going. And when he tests me, I will come out as pure as gold. For I have stayed on God's paths; I have followed his ways and not turned aside. I have not departed from his commands, but have treasured his words more than daily food."*

Even in the midst of great suffering, Job expressed his love for God's Word. The more we read and study the Bible, the more we realize how valuable it is in our quest for peace. I am convicted when I hear stories of those who long to read God's Word, but are unable to own a Bible. Many of us have multiple Bibles in our homes, yet we neglect to read the treasured words that God has given us.

As you read the following verses, record the reasons that we should consider God's Word a treasure.

Psalm 119:105 _____

Psalm 119:11 _____

Isaiah 55:11 _____

Hebrews 4:12 _____

In Matthew 4:4 (NLT) Jesus expresses the importance of God's Word saying, *People do not live by bread alone, but by every word that comes from the mouth of God.*

He declares the validity of God's Word in His prayer found in John 17:17 (NLT) *Make them holy by your truth; teach them your word, which is truth.*

Paul writes in his letter to the Colossians: *Let the message about Christ, in all its richness, fill your lives. Teach and counsel each other with all the wisdom he gives. Sing psalms and hymns and spiritual songs to God with thankful hearts.* Colossians 3:16

Then James gives this instruction: *But don't just listen to God's word. You must do what it says. Otherwise, you are only fooling yourselves.* James 1:22

An invitation is extended to each one of us in Philippians 4:6-9 (NLT)

Don't worry about anything; instead, pray about everything. Tell God what you need, and thank him for all he has done. Then you will experience God's peace, which exceeds anything we can understand. His peace will guard your hearts and minds as you live in Christ Jesus.

And now, dear brothers and sisters, one final thing. Fix your thoughts on what is true, and honorable, and right, and pure, and lovely, and admirable. Think about things that are excellent and worthy of praise. Keep putting into practice all you learned and received from me—everything you heard from me and saw me doing. Then the God of peace will be with you.

God's Blessing of Peace

God desires that we experience peace. Peace of heart, peace of mind, peace of spirit. In Numbers 6:22-23 we read the words God spoke to Moses, *"Tell Aaron and his sons, 'This is how you are to bless the Israelites.'"*

God wanted to communicate clearly to His people – and to you and me – His personal blessing. The words that follow in Numbers 6:24-26 (NLT) give us a glimpse of the incredible love, compassion and blessing God has for his people.

"May the LORD bless you and protect you. May the LORD smile on you and be gracious to you. May the LORD show you his favor and give you his peace."

What a beautiful picture of God's love. The assurance of God's care, His grace, His desire to make Himself known, personally – intimately as we look into His face – causing us to rest in the beauty of His blessing. Closing the blessing He offers to us that which all men seek – His peace.

Four Steps to Peace

This Bible study is a reflection of what I have experienced in a journey that has led me to a place of peace. Because it has transformed my life, my God given passion is to share this treasure with you. My desire is to encourage you to take these steps so that you, too, will experience God's perfect peace. The order of the steps have been presented in a specific manner because I have found that the first three steps, praise, repent, and acknowledge prepare me with the proper perspective to yield my needs to God. Each step is important, but can be taken as God leads.

I encourage you to PRAY continually.

P raise continually

R epent continually

A cknowledge continually

Y ield continually, and experience

Peace

The journey to peace, just as any other journey, takes time and perseverance. The destination is well worth it. Not only will you find that your life is transformed, you will leave a legacy of peace that will spill out on others.

My Prayer for You

I pray this prayer for you with the passion that Paul prayed for the Ephesians:

"When I think of all this, I fall to my knees and pray to the Father, the Creator of everything in heaven and on earth. I pray that from his glorious, unlimited resources he will empower you with inner strength through his Spirit. Then Christ will make his home in your hearts as you trust in him. Your roots will grow down into God's love and keep you strong. And may you have the power to understand, as all God's people should, how wide, how long, how high, and how deep his love is. May you experience the love of Christ, though it is too great to understand fully. Then you will be made complete with all the fullness of life and power that comes from God.

Now all glory to God, who is able, through his mighty power at work within us, to accomplish infinitely more than we might ask or think. Glory to him in the church and in Christ Jesus through all generations forever and ever! Amen." Ephesians 3:14-21 (NLT)

Taking the Steps

Praise

God is Faithful – worthy of trust; consistently reliable

Lamentations 3:22-23 (NLT) The faithful love of the LORD never ends! His mercies never cease. Great is his faithfulness; his mercies begin afresh each morning.

Psalm 89:8 (NLT) O LORD God of Heaven's Armies! Where is there anyone as mighty as you, O LORD? You are entirely faithful.

Deuteronomy 32:4 (NLT) He is the Rock; his deeds are perfect. Everything he does is just and fair. He is a faithful God who does no wrong; how just and upright he is!

I praise you, God for _____

Repent

1 John 1:9 (NLT) But if we confess our sins to him, he is faithful and just to forgive us our sins and to cleanse us from all wickedness.

I confess and turn from _____

Acknowledge

I thank you for showing your faithfulness in answered prayer. I thank you for

_____

Yield

2 Thessalonians 3:3,5 (NLT) But the Lord is faithful; he will strengthen you, _____, and guard you from the evil one. May the Lord lead your heart, _____, into a full understanding and expression of the love of God and the patient endurance that comes from Christ.

I pray for _____

_____

Prayer Journal

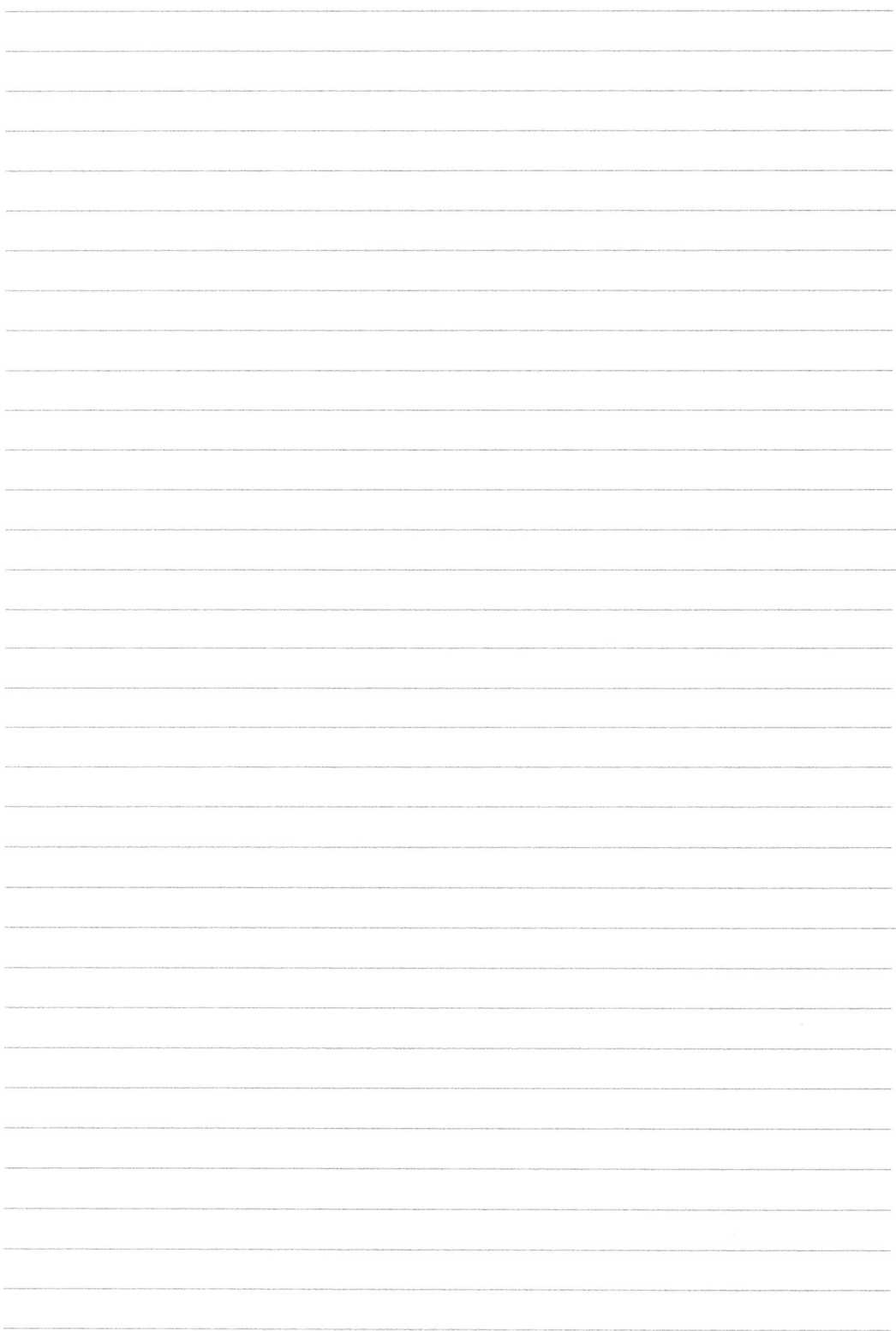

fully in focus

A Scriptural Collection

Illustrating the Attributes

of GOD

Carol Graves
www.FullyInFocus.com

fully in focus

Discovering the Fullness

of GOD

Learning to Fill the Empty Spaces
in the Journey of Life

Carol Graves

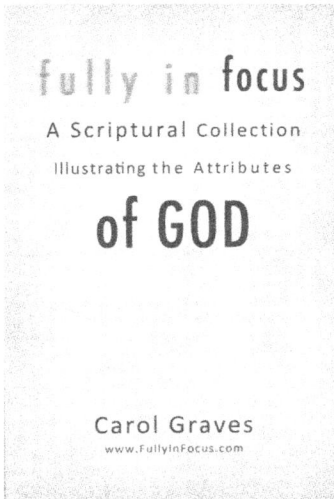

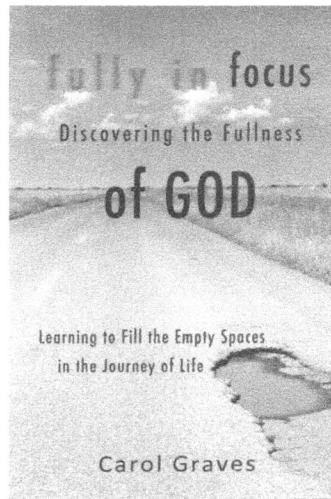

Companion Books

Carol Graves has written two devotional books each illustrating 52 attributes of God. The definitions, personal notes and Scripture references encourage a deeper knowledge of God's character. These helpful tools equip those who want to focus on the fullness of God as they experience the journey to peace.

Carol has also authored five children's books, each designed to teach young children about God and His gift of salvation. Titles include:

My First Glimpse of God

The Shining Star of Christmas

The Grumble Bug

The Girl Who Wanted a Friend

The Boy Who Said, "I Can't!"

All books are available for order at
www.fullyinfocus.com